FRAGRANCE IN THE GARDEN

FRAGRANCE IN

D. VAN NOSTRAND COMPANY, INC

THE GARDEN

By NORMAN TAYLOR

TORONTO • NEW YORK • LONDON

NEW YORK
D. Van Nostrand Company, Inc.
250 Fourth Avenue, New York 3

TORONTO
D. Van Nostrand Company (Canada), Ltd.
25 Hollinger Road, Toronto

LONDON
Macmillan & Company, Ltd.
St. Martin's Street, London, W.C. 2

Published simultaneously in Canada by
D. VAN NOSTRAND COMPANY (Canada), LTD.

Library of Congress Catalog Card No. 53-10390

PRINTED IN THE UNITED STATES OF AMERICA

Preface

The librarian of the best horticultural libı
recently told me that fragrance in the garder
our most pathetically handicapped—the blind.
and the form of flowers are but hearsay, but t
seems to enhance their sense of smell and henc
tion of flower scent is usually keener than ours

Although the book was not written fo
audience, if this book contributes in any measu
ment of the blind, it will have added cons
pleasure of having written it. They are like
souls who steal out to the garden in the night
that nature reserves for darkness some of our
scents.

In adopting the classification of flower odors
to perfumes, the book differs from others in t
are arranged by odors rather than in the mor
methods of recent books on fragrant plants. It
the method will add new interest to growing fr
and a better understanding of the significance o

Elmwood
Princess Anne, Maryland
Midsummer, 1953

Table of Contents

How to Use the Book

Nature scatters fragrance with an Olympian disregard for the experts—be they chemists, perfumers, or gardeners. Flower scent is hence so fortuitous that any scheme of arrangement seems hopeless, and would be completely so were it not for the fact that flower odors do conform to basic patterns.

This is not so simple as it sounds. Years of expert research by chemists, botanists, and perfumers finally have permitted us to arrange flower odors, and hence our fragrant gardens, according to the system evolved by Count Kerner von Marilaun, an Austrian botanist, and simplified, as here used, by F. A. Hampton, in his *The Scent of Flowers and Leaves,* first published in 1925.

It is hence urged upon the reader that he look over the first chapter especially. Here will be found the basic arrangement of flower odors, and from it one can plan what to use among the shrubs, trees, and vines in Chapter Two and the annuals or perennials in Chapter Three. Chapter Four is self-explanatory.

In the last three chapters will be found information on how to capture fragrance for the house, how to prepare perfume from flowers, and how to make a potpourri and sachet.

Chapter One

The Nature of Fragrance and How to Identify Some Types of It

Although perfumes are impossible to describe, there are certain *types* of them easily recognized, all of which are derived from the scents of flowers. Most of them, or so the chemists tell us, have been duplicated in the laboratory, to the despair of the discriminating, for natural fragrance is usually a subtle blending of several types of fragrance and the precise mixture baffles the scientist. He can analyze the floral oils, even give us horrendous formulas for the chemical compounds present in them, but no chemical magic or mixing of coal-tar derivatives has ever yet precisely imitated the intoxicating odor of the tuberose or jasmine—those pillars of French perfumery so essential that thousands of acres of southern France are covered with them.

For the gardener these main types of fragrance have more than academic interest. Everyone knows the difference between the scent of mignonette and a rose, even if we cannot describe either one. And the reason is that the mignonette and the rose, as do most garden flowers, belong to definite *types* of fragrance. Skillful gardeners, like skillful perfumers, can, with a few basic facts, blend fragrance for specially alluring or only mildly enticing effects. The trade names of perfumes—Tabu, Toujours Moi, My Sin, Joy, Fleur de Feu, Indiscret, Divine, Vol de Nuit—try desperately to capture the emotional effects produced by the complicated fragrance of a flower as simple as a violet, a rose, or the jasmine.

Nor have the coiners of such colorful names forgotten the basic lure of fragrance, which is sex—delicate or gross as the case may be, for even the vile odor of the skunk cabbage is a lure for those carrion-eaters who will complete its stinking nuptials. Far more subtle is the amazing development of fragrant moths and butterflies, whose scent closely matches the odor of the flowers they fertilize. The insect scent is definitely a sex characteristic, for without it the love life of these particular creatures would be far less enticing. For centuries the flower scent has been known as the lure that attracts the right sort of day-flying or night-flying insect to unite the male and female elements in a floral marriage indescribably fragrant.

Leaving out those scents that are repulsive, or of no interest to anyone, we can list six distinctly different *types* of fragrance that the gardener should know before planning the fragrant garden. Although modern chemistry cannot duplicate any of them exactly, it is to the laboratory that we owe the knowledge that certain chemicals are the basis for these typical flower scents. Those of interest to the gardener can be easily summarized thus:

1. Aminoid, generally having trimethylamine and propylamine as constituents.

This group is rather limited, and its odor is best typified by the hawthorn, pear, spirea, and elder. Many other flowers contain whiffs of it, but none of them is either sweet or heavy. Flowers in this group are fertilized by various species of flies and never by butterflies or night-flying moths. Most of them are spring-flowering.

2. Heavy, always containing benzyl acetate, indol, and methyl anthranilate.

A large group of extremely sweet-smelling flowers, some of them a little overpowering. The typical odor is that of the jasmine, but it is, in various blends, also found in mock-orange (*Philadelphus* or syringa), many lilies, tuberose, lilac, some honeysuckles, etc. A curious feature of the group is that the indol, which is always present, is also found in the end-products of animal putrefaction. It is the presence of indol in greater or less amounts which makes certain flowers in this group, notably *Philadelphus* (mock-orange or syringa), disturbing to some—as though sweetness and decay were mixed by nature as a warning. John Gerard in his famous herbal (1597) found syringa "too sweet, troubling and molesting the head in a strange manner."

Most of this group, which must be used with caution in the garden and especially as cut flowers, are fertilized by butterflies, and many of them, whose odor is perceptible only after dusk, are fertilized by night-flying moths. It is among these moths and butterflies that the extraordinary adaptation is found whereby the fragrance of the flower is almost precisely matched by that of the male insect visitor.

3. AROMATIC. The essential oils of this group contain eugenol, cinnamic alcohol, vanilla, and often others. The effect is nearly always spicy, as why shouldn't it be when the constituents may be blends of such heavily scented essences as those found in cinnamon, vanilla, cloves, and anise.

The typical flower of this type is the clove pink, but it contains many others, where blends of the different main constituents are pretty complex, particularly when some odors found in Group 2 (Heavy) are mixed with the aromatics. Some flowers are thus hard to classify as between this group and the last because they contain elements of both, notably hyacinth, heliotrope, night-scented stock, and *Nicotiana.* However, since none of the plants in Group 3 contains indol, the flavor of decay, which some find a bit overpowering in the mock-orange, is avoided.

Other flowers in the aromatic group, often blended with related essences, are certain species of rose, many pinks *(Dianthus),* primrose, cowslip, some species of *Clematis,* many orchids from the tropics, and the sweet-smelling *Gladiolus tristis.*

All the flowers in the aromatic group are fertilized by butterflies or moths, and the scent of all of them, with the possible exception of *Nicotiana,* is not so heavy nor heady nor sweet-cloying as those found in Group 2. The aromatics tend to be spicy, lively, and more cheery,—and quite definitely less sensual or downright sexy.

4. VIOLET. The essential oil derived from *Viola odorata* (the florist's violet) is characterized by irone, an oily, sweet-smelling compound from which the perfumers derive ionone, the basis of synthetic violet perfume.

The type flower is the violet, the elusiveness of whose odor is famous. There is no impact such as comes from the Heavy or Aromatic groups, for the flowers within the violet group are more delicate, and the scent of some of them has the curious faculty of running out on you. You smell them, and the scent appears to fade—it probably doesn't, but maybe our sense of smell is what really fades.

Outside the true *Viola odorata* and the Parma violet, the scent is not common, and only extremely faint in most wild violets. It is found among some species of iris, rather faintly (among other essences) in mignonette, and in a few tropical acacias.

5. Rose. The basis of the odor in all fragrant roses is geraniol, a highly complex substance containing oil of lemon, oil of orange, oil of bay leaves, etc.

Only the fragrant roses come within this group, except for one or two species of peony, the Oregon grape, an iris or two, and several tropical plants of little interest to the average northern gardener. The scent is never heavy, but it may be slightly aromatic or fruity.

It should be remembered that the "rose" scent is not found in all roses and that it varies in the roses that are fragrant, especially in some tea roses. The musk rose, the cabbage rose, and the old Provence rose *(Rosa gallica)* are thought by the experts to have a true "rose" perfume, but it may be a complex as difficult to untangle as are some of the hybrid roses that may or may not have any odor at all. It is certainly true that the plants from which the perfumers obtain the famous attar of rose are the damask rose and a variety of *Rosa alba,* known as *suaveolens,* which is much grown in southern France. Some modern roses have practically no scent, and these will be noted later so that we can omit them from the fragrant garden.

6. LEMON. As the name suggests, citral is the active ingredient of this odor, which is found in the lemon and in some other citrus fruits.

Among garden flowers it is not common (in the citrus fruits the odor is in an oil in the rind of the fruit), but some species of *Magnolia* have it as does the four-o'clock and the beautiful, little, white water lily, one of the most fragrant of all our native plants.

The lemon group of flowers has a fragrance a little sharp, somewhat lively, thought by some to be related to the "rose" scent, but scarcely ever heavy. It is rarely found pure in flowers, but is typical in the rind of lemon, the leaves of lemon verbena, and in some species of eucalyptus, balm, etc.

There are perhaps one or two other categories of flower scents, but their chemical constituents are not well known nor are there enough flowers in them to make it worth the gardener's while to clutter up his scheme with them. One of them comprises the musk-scented flowers, which, however, have nothing to do with the true animal musk of the perfumers. Another group is thought to have animal-like odors suggestive of cats, foxes, goats, and other creatures that have no place in the garden.

For the gardener in search of fragrance it will often be helpful to know where the different plants in subsequent chapters fall as to their fragrance. Wherever it is certainly known, each plant is segregated under a group number. These numbers, as outlined previously, will tell the gardener at least what type of fragrance to expect. If further details are wanted, reference should be made to the discussion of the six perfume types. They may be summarized here, together with the flower that typifies each group, as:

1. Aminoid—Hawthorn
2. Heavy—Jasmine
3. Aromatic—Clove pink
4. Violet—Violet
5. Rose—Rose
6. Lemon—Four-o'clock

No gardener should expect to find his favorite fragrance fitting precisely into any one of the six categories. Nature does not work that way. Each of the groups is characterized by some odor. A flower whose odor is nearest to the characteristic is then selected as the type of that group. For each group there are one or more chemical compounds chiefly responsible for the particular odor, and nearly all of these compounds have been chemically isolated from the fresh flowers. But none of this sophistication tells us one helpful word about the true nature of the fragrance of any particular flower, for its odor is a compound of many things. Some are guessed at by the chemists, some are dreamed up by the perfumers, but most of the secrets of fragrance are, one suspects, known only to God.

In spite of our ignorance as to the true nature of fragrance it is still possible for the planner of a fragrant garden to select the plant materials needed to make the garden a delight by day and an alluring intoxication at night. Reference to the key numbers, as outlined above, will help, and it is unfortunate that our knowledge is still too incomplete to supply these data for all the plants in the book. All of them are fragrant in various degrees, but it is not yet possible to assign all of them to the six main types of fragrance.

Concerning the hardiness and availability of the plants discussed in the subsequent chapters, all are perfectly hardy in the area of the United States which stretches from Boston-New York-Philadelphia westward, except those specially noted. The latter, unfortunately containing some of our most sweet-smelling plants, are not certainly hardy northward.

As to their availability, all the shrubs, trees, and woody vines are regularly carried in stock by most of the larger nurseries, and some of them must be sought from such firms, for small roadside stands may not have all the different sorts. For the bulbs, seeds, and plants of the perennials and annuals any good seedman's catalog will list them, and a good many of the plants can be had at most reasonably well-stocked roadside stands.

Cultural notes are omitted except where they are especially needed, for it can usually be assumed that the planner of a fragrant garden is beyond the kindergarten stage of horticulture. If such help is needed, the reader is referred to *Taylor's Encyclopedia of Gardening,* which has complete cultural notes for all the plants in this book and for several thousand others.

Chapter Two

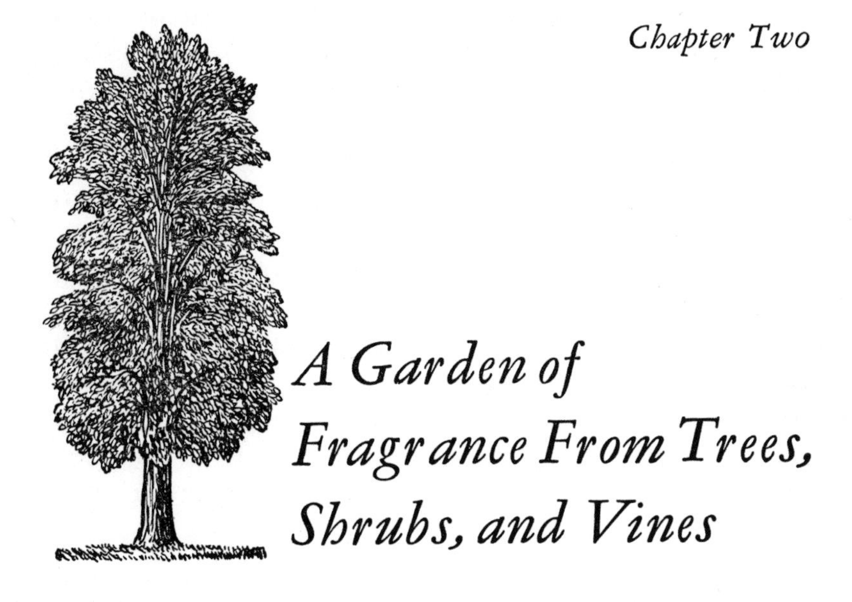

A Garden of Fragrance From Trees, Shrubs, and Vines

Any permanent fragrance in the garden must come from plants that are themselves relatively permanent, which means trees, shrubs, or woody vines. Grouped either by season of bloom or by the type of perfume they exhale, these woody plants can make any open window, patio, or porch a place of pure enchantment.

Because the plants are permanent, or at least should not be moved without good reason, it is well to study your surroundings rather carefully before planting any of the material to be listed. One of the first things to determine is the direction of prevailing summer winds. If you want fragrance wafted into the house, it is idle to place your plants so that the prevailing wind carries delicious scents toward the garage or across the street.

Once this direction is noted (the summer wind is from the southwest over much of the Atlantic seaboard), it is just as important to know when you want odors from your garden. Some of the shrubs and trees will be in bloom from early in March to late autumn. Do you want continuous perfume in the garden or are some weeks or months of less importance than others? Furthermore, how much fragrance do you want? The answers to these questions you alone can provide, but it is well to remember that fragrance, like color in the garden, can be overdone. It is one of the most charming of experiences to come suddenly upon a sweet-scented plant in a border. But what if the garden were crammed with them to the exclusion of other features? We can get too much fragrance, especially from those that belong to the *Heavy* or *Aromatic* types (as specified in Chapter One).

Furthermore, you should keep in mind, when plotting the location of anything as permanent as shrubs and trees, how much fragrance you want from the annuals and perennials treated in Chapter Three and, therefore, how much space must be allowed for them. Many of these herbaceous plants can be scattered in odd places—edges of borders, in the half shade of shrubs and trees, or as edging for foundation plantings.

Generally speaking it is just as sound to make a plan for fragrance as it is for color or for the development of any garden, large or small. The advantages are obvious—if for nothing else, that you can carry it out piecemeal and hence work toward a finished scheme rather than plant haphazardly with all the future adjustments and headaches that a planless garden usually entails. This procedure is necessary for the orderly development of a garden. (I can already hear the protests of some very good gardeners who delight in the wild confusion of some old gardens where color, fragrance, sentiment, and statuary are as delightfully mixed as their minds!)

Because fragrance is our chief object the woody plants below are arranged in the groups outlined in Chapter One, according to the *type* of perfume to be expected. Again it should be emphasized that scarcely any of the plants that belong to any one *type* will give the same fragrance as any other plant in the group. Nature has been lavish in her mixing of the different essences, the total result of which we know and love so much in the fragrance of jasmine, rose, lilac, and scores of others.

To help the reader make a selection, each plant will have notes as to when it will be in flower in the latitude of New York; for places north or south of this latitude, bloom can be expected from a few days to a week or two later or earlier, respectively. Also, proximity to cool seawater, as well as any elevation above 1000 feet, will retard the bloom of spring-flowering shrubs and trees.

Nearly all the most fragrant plants have good, well-known English common names and wherever these are unmistakable they are used. In cases of doubt, and in all for which there are no common names, we must fall back on the Latin names found in the catalogs. Whenever these are used, they must be followed exactly when it comes to ordering seeds or plants, because many large groups (iris, rose, peony, azalea, etc.) contain some fragrant kinds, whereas others are practically odorless.

1. AMINOID—TYPE FLOWER, HAWTHORN

Some time ago the writer was paddling a canoe along the wondrous edge of a tropical forest in the Amazon. Heavy with the scent of orchids and the odor of dank lianes, a new and especially sweet fragrance became dominant and almost overpowering as we rounded a bend in the lagoon—and came upon a dilapidated shed! It was full of tonka beans. One could no more analyze the fascinating odor than he could think up a formula for ambergris. It seemed a mixture of new-mown hay, vanilla, and some of the finest smoking mixtures. What tonka contains is coumarin, a wonderful compound used to flavor good tobaccos for pipe-smokers, to impart an odor to artificial vanilla, and to enhance perfume.

Many of the fragrant plants in this section owe their charm to whiffs of coumarin, which is, in more or less significant concentrations, found in many plants. Without going so far as the Amazon, one can get a hint of it from any freshly cut lawn, the mowing of which seems to release coumarin otherwise locked away in the uncut blades of grass.

Some of the plants below contain minute amounts of this quite magical compound, as well as the others mentioned in Chapter One. None of them has an overpowering scent, such as found in the next section, but the hawthorn was sweet and entrancing enough for Keats to have written:

> So I straightway went to pick a posy,
> Of luxurious May both white and rosy.

While the aminoid type of fragrance is found among quite a few plants, often in seeds, pods, leaves, or roots, the number of garden *flowers* that are in the group is pretty limited. It is found in apple and pear blossoms, and in some cherries, but except for these fruit trees there are only a few shrubs and trees for the fragrant garden.

HAWTHORN. A tree 10-20 feet high, blooming in May—hence the other common English name for it of *May*. It comes in white and pink forms and also double-flowered varieties are offered, but these are best avoided if one wants to be certain of fragrance. Not everyone likes the odor of hawthorn and perhaps because of this an old superstition grew up in England that its combination of bitter-almond, coumarin, and faintly fishy smell portended evil. Many simple rustics would never bring cut sprays into their cottages, for it was supposed to be followed by a death in the family. Most modern gardeners prefer to follow Keats, however, although it is certainly true that neither bees nor butterflies will touch hawthorn, leaving its fertilization to flies, for bees and butterflies like sweeter odors than that of the hawthorn. It is, of course, the plant around which grew up the picturesque rusticity of May Day and the Maypole.

BECHTEL'S CRAB. A beautiful, double-flowered crabapple, usually a shrub 8-10 feet high, but often tree-like, as its ancestor is a native tree in the central United States. The fruit is inedible; in May the plant is covered for about ten days with a riot of pink flowers that seem spicy, or rose-like, and thought by some to have a whiff of violets. It is, however, neither a heavy nor an overpowering fragrance.

MEADOWSWEET *(Spiraea alba)*. A native, almost weedy shrub, scarcely more than 3-4 feet high, with white flowers in midsummer. The odor is mild, redolent of the wild pastures in which it usually grows. It should not be confused with the

European meadowsweet, which is really an herb *(Filipendula ulmaria)* the odor of which is unpleasant to some, although Queen Elizabeth I used to strew the floors of her palace with it.

2. HEAVY—TYPE FLOWER, JASMINE

The heavy, alluring types of perfume immediately conjure up visions of Cleopatra or the Persians who carried their use to an extravagance and splendor never since attempted. Who today, no matter how prodigal, would drench the sails of a ship with perfume, as Cleopatra did, so that the very "winds were lovesick." Centuries later, Saadi, one of the immortal Persian poets, wrote in his *Gulistan:*

> Art Thou, then, musk or ambergris, I said;
> That by thy scent my soul is ravished?

It was the ancient world that brought the art of perfumery to a perfection it has perhaps never reached since. The Greeks, Romans, Arabs, Persians, and the Egyptians made such a cult of sweet-smelling essences that perfumed palaces, princes, kings, queens, mistresses, baths, and gardens were a commonplace. It is some compensation that we can cultivate some of the very plants used by the ancients for making fragrant everything from temple worship to the bacchanalia.

It is no accident that the chief flower they used in the extraction of their heavy, languorous, sensual and sex-exciting perfumes should be a sprawling or half-climbing shrub with perhaps the sweetest-smelling blooms in the world—the jasmine. It was originally native in the region from Persia and Arabia to China. We moderns, however, have one advantage over the ancients. Their world did not know the existence of many other plants that exploration and discovery have added to our gardens, some of which by their fragrance emphatically belong with the jasmine among the *heavy* or sensuous types of scent. In addition to the shrubs and trees that will be listed, there are other heavily scented plants found in Chapter Three (annuals and perennials)—notably the tuberose.

In planting any of them the gardener ought to decide whether he wants the languorous, seductive scents of some of these plants wafted into windows, onto the porch, or into some secluded patio. Or is it better and maybe safer to scatter them in more open places where allurement will be tempered by wind or the proximity of less ravishing plants? Only individual tastes can dictate such decisions, for they are more emotional than horticultural.

With the emotional dangers in view, the reader is now at liberty to choose these heavily scented plants to suit his mood, for all of them are of easy culture, and their flowering period stretches from February to October.

FEBRUARY, MARCH, AND APRIL

The earliest blooming of all fragrant shrubs and trees is a Chinese, shrubby honeysuckle *(Lonicera fragrantissima),* 8-10 feet high, evergreen in the South, but losing most of its leaves in winter around New York, north of which it is not certainly hardy. Its rather small, white flowers open in greatest profusion in January along the Gulf Coast, in February in Richmond, and by March in Philadelphia. Its bloom, which is so sweet-smelling as to be nearly overpowering, is sometimes blasted by late frosts in the north. If grown north of New York, it definitely needs protection.

Perhaps even more powerfully scented is the tea olive *(Osmanthus fragrans),* dear to the hearts of Southern belles, and certainly not hardy much north of Norfolk or the Eastern Shore of Maryland and Virginia. It is a lustrous, evergreen shrub or small tree, a native of Southeastern Asia, never more than 25 feet high, and more often shrub-like. Flowers, inconspicuous, but extraordinarily fragrant, usually bloom about April or earlier southward. A more hardy, but somewhat less fragrant relative, is *Osmanthus ilicifolius* from Japan. It will stand the climate as far north as Wilmington, Delaware, and flowers in June or early July.

In the latter part of March or early April, there are two species of *Daphne* that belong in all fragrant gardens from Boston southward. One is the mezereon *(Daphne mezereum),* a shrub 18-36 inches high, covered with rosy-lilac flowers before the leaves unfold. An evergreen relative, sometimes called garland-flower *(Daphne cneorum),* is even lower, forms dense mats and hence is useful as a ground cover. Its flowers are very fragrant and pink. It may need to be covered with leaves in the North, but is generally perfectly hardy as far north as Boston.

Ever since 1902 the garden world has been enchanted with a small shrub from Korea, which in spite of its popularity still has no valid common name. It is or should be known to all gardeners as *Viburnum carlesi* and scarcely exceeds 3-4 feet in height. In April, or in the North in early May, it is covered with a profusion of small, white flowers in dense clusters that are almost dangerously fragrant. It is suited to all soils and all climates up to Canada and blooms with the unfolding of the leaves. Besides its heavy odor there appears to be mixed with the main scent a whiff of aromatic or spicy, almost clove-like, fragrance, making this Korean beauty a match almost for jasmine.

MAY

HONEYSUCKLE. Almost all the common vines of this group are extremely fragrant, most of them a bit rampant and hence to be used with caution in small gardens. For, notwithstanding their perfume, they may become a nuisance. Some of the vines, for instance, may completely smother neighboring shrubs. Since most of the vines will bloom throughout the season, they are valuable, if one curbs their tendency to monopolize too much space. Most of them are pale yellow, merging into orange and red.

Among bush honeysuckles, which never capture too much space, there are two shrubs that should be in any fragrant garden, although neither of them has yet acquired a common name. *Lonicera syringantha,* from China, is 5-8 feet high and bears a profusion of rather small, rosy-lilac flowers, most sweetly smelling, almost hyacinth-like in their perfume. A lower, round-headed relative, *Lonicera thibetica,* from western China, has purplish-rose flowers, just as fragrant and, like *Lonicera syringantha,* perfectly hardy. For other honeysuckles, see *Aromatic* (Section 3 of this chapter).

LILAC. Most old gardens contain the venerable, single-flowered lilac, an original inhabitant of southeastern Europe, but now grown everywhere. It is this flower that has inspired the poets—from the Persians, who knew it well, on to John Masefield and his "In Lilac Time." Its fragrance is very heavy, and to some distinctly cloying.

This old, single-flowered favorite, mostly 8-15 feet high, has been largely replaced by hundreds of hybrids, because of the genius of Belgian and especially French hybridists. Some are single-flowered, some double, and their color ranges from white to deep lavender-blue. They are undeniably finer plants than their ancestors, but of the hundreds of named sorts, not all are fragrant, and some retain the unpleasant odor of their close relative—the privet.

Among the French hybrid lilacs, it is therefore necessary to choose varieties with care. A dozen of those that are notably fragrant and easily procurable will be all that the average gardener needs, leaving to the lilac specialists the task of sifting out the more than 250 named forms that are offered in the United States. The best (that is, most fragrant and easily procurable from ordinary sources) are:

Lamartine (pink, single-flowered)
Miss Ellen Willmott (white, double-flowered)
Vestal (white, single-flowered)
Congo (deep, purplish-red, single-flowered)
Waldeck Rousseau (rosy-lilac, double-flowered)
Leon Gambetta (rose-salmon, single-flowered)
De Saussure (purple-red, double-flowered)
President Lincoln (blue, single-flowered)
Diderot (claret-purple, single-flowered)
Ludwig Spaeth (red, single-flowered)
President Grevy (blue, double-flowered)

In addition to these fragrant hybrid lilacs there are some species of lilac that ought to be in any fragrant garden, but there are pitfalls in the genus *Syringa* to which all lilacs belong. Not all species are fragrant and some have the objectionable privet odor. Among the available species, which must be ordered by their Latin names, the following are fragrant, and it would be safer to ignore the other nonfragrant or disagreeably scented lilacs. All those below are single-flowered.

Syringa vulgaris, 8-15 feet, lilac-lavender, the original and oldest lilac in cultivation. From it and the next, many of the hybrids have been derived.

Syringa persica, 5-6 feet, pale lilac, often called the Persian lilac, although it is native from Persia to China. The parent of many hybrids.

Syringa oblata, 8-12 feet, pale lilac, and a native of China. Blooms a fortnight before the common lilac.

Syringa chinensis, 8-15 feet, purplish lilac. A hybrid between the first and second species, developed about 1777 in France long before the modern French hybrids were thought of.

There is, in addition to the honeysuckles and lilacs, a shrub that demands the loyalty of all who seek fragrance in the Southern garden. It is likely to bloom toward the end of May or early in June and is known as *Viburnum odoratissimum.* It is found wild from India to Japan and is a shrub 7-10 feet high. It is closely related to *Viburnum carlesi,* already noted under the shrubs blooming in April, but differs in an important respect. Its fragrance, although very sweet and properly classed with the heavy scents, has also a distinct tincture of the aminoid (see Chapter One). Unfortunately, it is not certainly hardy north of Norfolk or Washington.

JUNE

Three extremely fragrant woody plants bloom in June, and all of them will completely scent any garden, particularly on still, damp days. One is the famous lime tree of Europe, which is really a linden; the other two are shrubs.

LINDEN. Beautiful shade trees, 60-90 feet high, the foliage so dense that little will grow under a full-grown tree. They are always called lime trees in Europe, but our American species are best known as basswood. Toward the first or middle part of June, the trees are covered with greenish-yellow flowers the nectar of which is a favorite of bees.

Their fragrance is famous, but to be sure of the best species it is better to plant the small-leaved European linden, for it is perhaps the most alluringly fragrant of all large trees. Somewhat less fragrant is the native American linden, with much larger leaves. Both trees, besides their heavy, sweet odor, have a dash of the spicy fragrance found among the more aromatic odors in the next section. Both lindens are perfectly hardy.

OLEASTER OR RUSSIAN OLIVE *(Elaeagnus angustifolius)*. A shrub or small tree 10-20 feet high, of the Mediterranean Region, called by the Portuguese the Tree of Paradise because of its extraordinarily fragrant yellow flowers. These are relatively small and inconspicuous, half hidden by the leaves, but exhaling such a perfume that maidens are said to blush with expectancy and brides with memory. It is one of the hardiest of all shrubs, differing in this respect from a later-flowering relative to be noted later.

MOCK-ORANGE OR SYRINGA. There are several different kinds and it is safer to order by the Latin name of *Philadelphus coronarius*. A native of southeastern Europe and adjacent Asia, it has been famous for its perfume for centuries. The flowers are white and waxy and suggest orange blossoms both in texture and odor, although many gardeners are disturbed by its cloying sweetness. Almost no plant in this book has such conflicting reports as this mock-orange. In addition to those already cited (Chapter One, in the section on *Heavy* fragrance), various experts have said it smells like a mixture of pineapple and orange blossoms, while one writer likens its odor to that of cucumbers. Some gardeners will not have the mock-orange at any price; whether because it is too sweet or too disturbing is not clear. In any event, it is better planted away from the house. So popular has it become that there are several named varieties offered. Those easily available include Golden, Dwarf Sweet, and Double.

MIDSUMMER

Charles Dickens once wrote that the jasmine is "the Isis of flowers," and that we should "crown the jasmine the empress and queen" of all flowers. Cleopatra thought so, as have the nabobs of India, the contemplative Persians, and even the staid Dioscorides. As physician to Anthony and Cleopatra, he found jasmine a symbol of their stormy passion as it has ever since been endeared to the hearts of countless millions. Perhaps the most heavily perfumed of all flowers, it is no wonder that garlands of it were once worn by brides, before orange blossoms became artificially available. No perfumer has ever exactly matched its incomparable scent.

Most unfortunately, northern gardeners cannot safely grow the true jasmine of story, legend, romance, and the perfumers. To distinguish it from the several other species of jasmine grown here, it is therefore necessary to specify the true jasmine as *Jasminum officinale* when ordering it, and it will be carried only by southern or California firms. A native from Persia, through India to China, this most fragrant of all shrubs is not safe to grow north of the southern part of the Eastern Shore of Maryland and Virginia, for while it will stand a little frost it emphatically will not endure protracted cold weather.

The plant is by no means a sturdy shrub, for its rather weak stems have a tendency to sprawl and, especially in the South, to clamber up walls. It may grow to 40 feet if given support, and some of it festoons the balconies of houses near the Battery in Charleston. Late in June or more likely in July-August, it bears a somewhat scattered bloom of white, chalice-like flowers.

For those to whom the true jasmine is climatically impossible there are fair compensations among its relatives. Of these *Jasminum nudiflorum,* a low shrub with yellow flowers in February-March, is hardy up to New York, but does not compare with the true jasmine in odor. Somewhat less hardy, but more fragrant species, all with yellow flowers, are *Jasminum floridum* and *Jasminum sambac,* the flowers of the latter used by the Chinese to flavor jasmine tea. Both are not safe to grow north of Washington. There is still another jasmine noted under Aromatic (Section 3 of this chapter).

Another midsummer bloomer is our native sweet pepper-bush, *(Clethra alnifolia),* common throughout the eastern United States and easily cultivated. It grows 3-5 feet high and bears terminal, spire-like clusters of deliciously scented white flowers. It can be grown anywhere in a variety of soils. Not so fragrant as jasmine, it suggests the odor of that incomparable plant, although *Clethra* has also a whiff of something aromatic or spicy, and some catch a breath of lilac in its odor.

AUTUMN

Quite naturally autumn is the time of waning fragrance, soon to usher in sere winter. Doubly welcome consequently is an extremely fragrant shrub from Japan, *Elaeagnus pungens,* which grows 10-15 feet high in the South, but less than this as it approaches the northern limit of its possible culture, which is between Washington and Richmond, although it is apparently safe along the Chesapeake coast of the Eastern Shore from

Maryland southward. Its quite inconspicuous flowers appear in October and provide a delightful autumnal odor of spicy pungency, mixed with more languorous fragrance.

3. AROMATIC—TYPE FLOWER, CLOVE PINK

When the Dutch once burned a warehouse full of spices, the air over Amsterdam was redolent of the East. For the Dutch East India Company then traded at the Moluccas, Celebes, Java, Sumatra, and Borneo, and some of the group became known as the Spice Islands. Romantic, odorous, and half-savage, the islands became famous as the source of nearly all the spices in the world. Cloves, nutmeg, ginger, pepper, mace, camphor, cinnamon, turmeric, and cardamons—what memories they evoke of rich foods, fine wines, pleasant dinners, and always a haunting sense of places most of us have never seen.

Like so many odors, "spicy" is impossible to describe. Instantly recognized, it defies definition and we fall back upon the known fact that spices are variously aromatic and that many flower scents contain this combination of scents. Many of them are herbs, like the clove pink and some kinds of carnations. All of these will be found in Chapter Three. Here we are concerned only with the trees, shrubs, and woody vines the flowers of which have a definitely aromatic or spicy fragrance.

Unlike those in Section 2 (Heavy) the aromatic fragrance of the plants below is neither sensual nor sex-exciting, except for a few which contain elements of both the heavy and aromatic types of fragrance. They charm rather than allure, and the gardener can plant them accordingly.

TREES

CATALPA. Medium-sized, quick-growing trees with profuse flower clusters in early summer. Of the several sorts grown in this country *Catalpa ovata,* from eastern Asia, is the most fragrant, honey-scented, but with a whiff of heavy odor suggesting the linden. The American *Catalpa speciosa* is considerably less fragrant.

SOURWOOD *(Oxydendrum arboreum).* A native tree, wild from Pennsylvania southward, with curiously bitter leaves and wood—hence its common name, often replaced by sorrel-tree. It reaches 20-30 feet in the wild, but generally less as cultivated, and in midsummer it is covered by hanging clusters of small, bell-shaped flowers with a decidedly aromatic fragrance. The tree is not well enough known to the garden public, but is carried by many nurserymen.

SHRUBS

Scarcely anyone expects garden fragrance in February, and consequently two shrubs from temperate eastern Asia, of the witch-hazel tribe are most welcome. Both bear yellow flowers like our native witch-hazel, but are much more fragrant, and as in ours have solitary flowers on naked, leafless twigs. As there are several other, and practically scentless, plants in the group, it is best to order them by their Latin names. *Hamamelis mollis* is a true witch-hazel from China; the other, from Japan, is *Corylopsis pauciflora,* a close relative of the witch-hazel. If you have room for only one, it is better to choose the latter.

Another winter-flowering Chinese shrub, very popular in the South, where it may bloom all winter, is *Chimonanthus praecox,* 8-10 feet high and evergreen along the Gulf Coast,

Northward it loses most of its leaves and is not hardy above Wilmington, Delaware, and not always there if the winter is severe. Its yellow flowers have a delicious spicy odor, with heavy overtones of a hyacinth-like fragrance.

Shrubs with more usual flowering periods include three that bloom in the spring, and four in midsummer.

SPRING FLOWERING

FLOWERING CURRANT, 6-8 feet high, its reddish-yellow blossoms without apparent odor unless cut sprays are taken into the house, when it will be deliciously spicy.

HONEYSUCKLE *(Lonicera heckrotti)*, a rather sprawling bush-honeysuckle, its extremely fragrant, purple flowers scented only at night. Like the honeysuckles mentioned at Section 2 (Heavy) it has a languorous odor, mixed in this case by a tinge of some aromatic essence; the combination is intoxicating.

CAROLINA ALLSPICE, 4-8 feet, and in June rather sparsely covered by deep chocolate or purple-brown flowers, so spicy that the plant has been variously callec Sweet-shrub, Sweet-scented Shrub, and Strawberry Shrub. It actually has a combination of fruit scent, especially pineapple, mixed with wine and camphor. No wonder children love to crush it among their clothes.

MIDSUMMER FLOWERING

GARDENIA. Not many gardeners ever think that the gardenia of the florists, perhaps the most popular of all corsage flowers, can be grown anywhere in the United States, outside of the greenhouse. But a variety of it, which must be carefully specified as *Gardenia jasminoides fortuniana* (in some catalogs it will be called *Gardenia veitchi),* can be grown outdoors from southern Maryland to the Gulf Coast. It is a handsome, broad-leaved evergreen shrub, 4-10 feet high, and bears its waxy, white, highly spicy blooms nearly all summer. For greatest fragrance and largest blooms it pays to pinch off all but a few blooms from each branch.

ITALIAN JASMINE *(Jasminum humile).* A loosely spreading, half-evergreen shrub with handsome, golden-yellow flowers that are nearly, but not quite, as fragrant as the true jasmine, which is noted as *Heavy* (Section 2 of this chapter). The Italian jasmine is a little hardier than the true jasmine, being safe to grow outdoors from Delaware and Cape May to the Gulf Coast. Besides its heavy, sweet odor, there is a spicy or aromatic element in its nearly overpowering fragrance.

BUTTERFLY-BUSH. Of these very showy midsummer-flowering shrubs the only one worth considering is *Buddleia davidi* from China, which, besides its aromatic odor, has a mixture of scents allied to those in hyacinth and lilac. It grows 4-10 feet high and bears handsome spikes of lavender-lilac flowers. In the north, it often is killed to the ground in winter, but next season's shoots bloom in spite of this and are just as fragrant.

BUTTON-BUSH, 5-12 feet high and common everywhere in the Eastern states, especially in swamps. It will grow in any ordinary garden soil, and its ball-like clusters of small, white flowers have a spicy or aromatic, but not strong fragrance, which is enticing but scarcely exciting.

WOODY VINES

One of the surest ways to bring fragrance into the house is to frame a window or doorway with sweet-smelling vines.

Among the spicy or aromatic group of fragrance only two vines seem of much significance, but both of them should have a place in any garden. Clematis, particularly, has a decidedly heady or sultry fragrance.

CLEMATIS. Beautiful and often showy woody vines, most of them so little known that they have no common names. Of the two-score species cultivated in the United States, only those below are fragrant enough to be worth including here. All are readily available.

Clematis recta, 2-5 feet high. Flowers white, in midsummer.

Clematis montana and its variety *rubens,* 10-20 feet high and a showy vine. Flowers white, except in the variety *rubens* where they are pink. Both bloom in May.

Clematis paniculata, the Japanese clematis, and a stout climber which may reach 30 feet. Flowers white. September-October.

Clematis crispa, often called blue jasmine because of its sweet jasmine-like fragrance. It is a shrubby or sprawling vine, 6-9 feet high, with bluish or bluish-purple flowers in midsummer, and often into September.

Most of the much more showy clematis hybrids, some of whose flowers are 4-6 inches across, have no fragrance.

HONEYSUCKLE *(Lonicera periclymenum).* An Old World woodbine sometimes climbing up to 20 feet, its yellowish-white, sometimes red-tinged flowers fragrant only at night. The scent is indescribably sweet, tinged with a spicy or aromatic odor which makes its flowers a delight to the young, but as one Englishman said of another vine "almost too rich and sweet for any respectably middle-aged liver!" For other honeysuckles, still more intoxicating, see *Heavy* (Section 2 of this chapter).

4. VIOLET—TYPE FLOWER, THE FLORIST'S VIOLET

The elusive scent of the violet is practically unknown among hardy shrubs and trees, although it has been detected in some subtropical acacias. For herbaceous plants that have it, see Chapter Three.

5. ROSE—TYPE FLOWER, ROSE

The rose type of fragrance, dictated mostly by the compound *geraniol,* is found in few other plants, and apparently among no woody ones, except the rose itself and the Oregon grape. The latter is a kind of barberry from our Pacific Coast, but perfectly hardy here. It is a spiny-leaved evergreen shrub, 4-8 feet high, with an erect cluster of yellow flowers that smell partly of the rose, somewhat fruity, and some have called it almost animal or musk-like in odor. Although a useful and handsome broad-leaved evergreen, its scent does not compare with that queen of all flowers.

The fragrance of the rose is so precious that roses have always been the most popular plants on earth. So many kinds were known to the Greeks and Romans that it took books to describe them. Perhaps a better gauge of their love of its scent is found among their customs, especially among the patricians. For the bacchanalia they would strew the floor of their palace with thousands of fresh rose petals, and release doves to fly above the heads of their guests—the birds having been sprayed with rose-water. Garlands of roses were strung along the walls, over statues and fountains, and potted roses framed such strategic nooks as their love couches.

It did not take the rose twenty centuries to recover from this debauchery, become respectable, and by the Middle Ages a symbol of purity, beauty, constancy and heaven knows how many other virtues. Today, judging by the receipts of florists' flowers in all our large cities, it is demanded more frequently than all other flowers, and in winter by more than all the rest put together.

For the hardy garden of fragrance the rose is a bit of a problem. Although nearly all wild *species* of rose are more or less fragrant, some are outstandingly so. Then there are several thousand named *varieties* of roses, many of which have lost practically all odor. To make a reasonable selection from this mass of material demands drastic restriction, and those mentioned below are among the best to choose from for fragrance. Other kinds, of course, are fragrant, in varying degrees. With the limited space that most of us can give to them, however, why not confine ourselves to those known to be among the sweetest-smelling varieties?

Not all of them will have the true "rose" scent (see Chapter One), for modern roses have a complex ancestry. Tea roses, for instance, were mostly derived from a Chinese species thought to have the odor of tea leaves—hence a little spicy; others have the blood in them of wild species that have a quite definite fruity fragrance. Others are tinged with lemon, some smell faintly of cinnamon, and should perhaps be classed with *Aromatic* (Section 3 in this chapter). Also, among the hundreds of varieties of hybrid roses, there appears to be some relation between color and fragrance. The deeper the red, the more pronounced the "rose" odor, while fragrance appears to fade as the reds become lighter, and fade still more in the frankly pink roses. Yellow roses are least likely to have a definite odor, while some white roses are very fragrant, especially the Cherokee rose which almost suggests the gardenia. Unfortunately, the Cherokee rose, the state flower of Georgia, is not hardy in the north.

Although not many modern gardeners have space or inclination to grow *species* roses, for the various types of hybrids are so much showier, it should not be forgotten that these species of rose were often the parents of the ancestors of many showy modern roses, some of which have, by gaining size and wonderful texture, lost nearly all their fragrance. Then, too, some of these old species of *Rosa* (which is the generic name of all roses) have a charm, often a dash of elegance; but most of all they have carried the fragrance of the rose for thousands of years without dilution and without the contamination that is inherent in rose genetics.

Of the three dozen species of *Rosa* known to be in cultivation those most worth growing, considering only their fragrance, might be the following. Unfortunately *Rosa alba,* a variety of which is a leading source of attar of roses in France, is all but unknown in this country. All those below, however, are readily available from many nurseries.

ROSE SPECIES

CABBAGE ROSE *(Rosa centifolia).* 4-6 feet high and upright. Flowers double, pink, nearly 3 inches wide. One of the oldest roses in cultivation and a variety of it is the moss rose which has sticky and "mossy" flower stalks.

CHINA ROSE *(Rosa chinensis).* 2-3 feet high and partly evergreen. Flowers single in the wild type, about 2 inches wide, crimson, pink, or even white in some forms. Not certainly hardy north of Norfolk, Virginia. Its fragrance has been bequeathed to many modern roses, notably the Manetti, Fairy Rose, Green Rose, etc.

DAMASK ROSE *(Rosa damascena)*. 4-8 feet high and erect. Flowers double, red or pink, rather small, but in loose clusters, very fragrant. A variety of it is the famous York and Lancaster rose, worn by opposite sides in the "War of the Roses." The damask rose is one of the sources of attar of roses.

PROVENCE or FRENCH ROSE *(Rosa gallica)*. 3-4 feet high and upright. Flowers solitary, single, pink or crimson, nearly 3 inches wide. This is one of the roses the petals of which seem to increase their fragrance after drying.

HIMALAYAN MUSK ROSE *(Rosa brunoni)*. Partially climbing and very prickly. Flowers white, 2 inches wide, with a musky fragrance, and in many-flowered clusters. Not certainly hardy north of Norfolk, or possibly to Washington, D. C. The true musk rose *(Rosa moschata)* of the Mediterranean region is practically unknown in the United States.

JAPANESE ROSE *(Rosa rugosa)*. 4-6 feet high and, if allowed to spread, making clumps 10-20 feet wide. Flowers single, red or white, with a delicious fruity odor. It grows perfectly along the seacoast. Double-flowered forms are known, but are best avoided if one insists on fragrance.

The foregoing, to the experts, may seem a meager list of *species* roses, but it has been deliberately restricted because most gardeners prefer the modern and very beautiful *hybrid* roses, of which the varieties are numbered in thousands, and over 1300 are actually available from the nurseries in the United States. A selection of the fragrant kinds, from such a huge mass of material, would be impossible were it not for the patient records kept by the American Rose Society and by many private growers.

All that space permits here is to list two dozen of these roses that are outstandingly fragrant, giving the class to which they belong, and the color of their flowers. Many fragrant roses, and some that are near-fragrant have had to be omitted, and some favorites may be missing—to the distress of those who for years may have cherished the rare odor of some variety but not always knowing its correct name or its general availability. All those below are to be found in any good nursery catalog, or if not, in those who specialize in roses. Among the latter are Bobbink and Atkins, Rutherford, New Jersey; Jackson and Perkins, Newark, New York; Conard and Pyle, West Grove, Pennsylvania; Kohankie and Son, Painesville, Ohio; C. H. Stocking Co., San José, California; Rosemont Nurseries, Tyler, Texas and A P R Roses, Inc., Tyler, Texas.

TWO DOZEN
FRAGRANT ROSE VARIETIES

Name	*Class*	*Color*
Captain Hayward	Hybrid Perpetual	Crimson
Climbing American Beauty	Climbing	Red
*Crimson Glory	Hybrid Tea	Crimson
Donald Prior	Floribunda	Red
*Etoile de Hollande	Hybrid Tea	Red
Florence Izzard	Hybrid Tea	Yellow
General Jacqueminot	Hybrid Perpetual	Crimson
George Arends	Hybrid Perpetual	Pink
Geranium Red	Floribunda	Red
Golden Dawn	Hybrid Tea	Yellow
Horace McFarland	Hybrid Tea	Salmon
Mary Margaret McBride	Hybrid Tea	Dark pink

*These varieties also come as climbers.

Mirandy	Hybrid Tea	Red
Mrs. Dunlop Best	Hybrid Tea	Yellow
Mrs. Pierre S. DuPont	Hybrid Tea	Golden yellow
Paul's Lemon Pillar	Climbing	Yellow
*Radiance	Hybrid Tea	Pink
*Red Radiance	Hybrid Tea	Red
Rubaiyat	Hybrid Tea	Crimson
Soleil d'Or	Hybrid Perpetual	Apricot
Signora	Hybrid Tea	Orange-salmon
The Doctor	Hybrid Tea	Pink
Vogue	Floribunda	Cherry-coral

*These varieties also come as climbers.

It would, of course, be idle to claim that these were the only two dozen hybrid roses that are fragrant. But they have been chosen because of their availability and their performance as to fragrance. Some of them, particularly among the hybrid tea roses, have a tendency to withhold their fragrance if it is hot, dry, and windy and are hence most charming in the quiet, windless hours. Some, also, are more fragrant just as they open; others only when full-blown. Your local conditions of shelter from winds, soil type, care, etc., will reveal these individual characteristics in a year or two. Also none of the two dozen will have such a consistently fine "rose" scent as the species roses mentioned earlier.

6. LEMON—TYPE FLOWER, FOUR-O'CLOCK

Lemons from Italy have such a delicious scent that many cooks and some Martini mixers prefer their spicy, lemony flavor, and hence odor, to any other of the citrus tribe. Citral, the dominant compound responsible for their highly pleasing odor, is, however, rather rare among the flowers that can be grown outdoors here. It is prominent in the four-o'clock and a few other herbaceous plants to be found in Chapter Three, as well as in the shrubs, trees, and vines mentioned below.

As in other flower scents this group is impossible to define without referring to something else—the oil found in the rind of a good Italian lemon plus a faint mixture of spicy or even aromatic scents. Orange blossoms may be in this group, but many believe its almost overpowering odor entitles it to inclusion among the *Heavy* scents (see Section 2 of this chapter). In any event, oranges cannot be grown anywhere in the North.

Among the shrubs and trees that are perfectly hardy in the North and certainly have the characteristic odor of the group are certain species of *Magnolia.* Of these the following are available and hardy in the North, except for the evergreen magnolia, which is the finest of the lot.

STAR MAGNOLIA *(Magnolia stellata).* 5-10 feet. A beautiful, rather spreading shrub, covered with star-like white flowers that unfold in early April before the leaves expand and are sometimes caught by late frosts. This, however, does not hurt the plant which will bloom the next year. It is caught by such late frosts about one year in six in the vicinity of New York; more often in Boston.

SWAMP LAUREL *(Magnolia virginiana).* 6-8 feet, but often a tree in the South and one of our most fragrant native shrubs. Flowers white in June. The plant is evergreen in the South, and nearly so in the North. Native in swamps from Rhode Island to Florida, but can be grown in ordinary garden soil.

EVERGREEN MAGNOLIA *(Magnolia grandiflora).* A magnificent tree, 60-80 feet high with showy, dark green, evergreen leaves. In June it bears enormous white flowers (6-8 inches across), and it is by far our most showy tree that is fragrant.

Unfortunately it is not certainly hardy north of Washington, D. C. (where there are fine specimens) and up the Eastern Shore (Virginia, Maryland, and Delaware) to Dover, Delaware. There is a large tree of it on a street in Brooklyn, N. Y.! But that does not mean that it can be grown safely much north of Delaware.

Only two other plants are in this group with lemon-scented flowers.

VIRGINIA WILLOW *(Itea virginica)*. 3-5 feet and a native shrub from New Jersey to Florida. In June or early July it bears finger-shaped clusters of small, white, beautifully fragrant flowers. Although it grows naturally in moist or swampy places, it can be grown in any good garden soil from Boston southward.

AKEBIA QUINATA, an Asiatic woody vine, often reaching a height of 15-20 feet with almost evergreen leaves. Flowers purplish-brown, rather inconspicuous, blooming in May at night and magnolia-scented. It is not certainly hardy north of Boston, but often above this along the coast.

For those who like to mix their fragrance in the garden with the fastidious taste that a good cook uses in making a culinary masterpiece, the shrubs, trees, and vines in the foregoing six types of fragrance will provide the ingredients. But the odor of some flowers defies classification, perhaps because it is too complicated, but mostly because the scientists have not yet found the ingredients that are responsible for the scent. This needs to deter no one from growing the plants listed below, for all are delightfully fragrant in spite of our ignorance of the cause. Of the many shrubs and trees whose odors have defied the researches of the scientists, the following seem worthy of culture in any fragrant garden:

STORAX *(Styrax japonica)*. A tree, 10-30 feet high, but often shrub-like. Flowers, bell-like, white, in finger-shaped clusters in late June or early July.

GORDONIA ALATAMAHA, a shrub or small tree, with evergeen or nearly evergreen leaves, native in Georgia, but now known only in cultivation, for no wild plants have been seen since its discovery, before 1800. Flowers cup-like, white, very fragrant, about 3½ inches across, and blooming in September or October. One of the most interesting of all native shrubs, as it was recently, but erroneously, "re-discovered." Some catalogs use the name *Franklinia* for it.

SWAMP HONEYSUCKLE *(Azalea viscosa)*. A shrub, 6-10 feet high, and native in the Eastern states. Flowers white or pink, in June, honey-scented, but not strongly so. Several other native azaleas are similarly fragrant, but a good many of the far more showy hybrid azaleas and their close relatives, the rhododendrons, are not notable for fragrance.

SYMPLOCOS PANICULATUS. A shrub 10-12 feet high and often tree-like. Flowers, small, white, in clusters, and blooming in May, followed by bright blue fruit.

SPANISH BROOM *(Spartium junceum)*. An almost leafless, rush-like shrub 6-8 feet high, its very fragrant, pea-like yellow flowers blooming all summer. It is not certainly hardy north of Norfolk, Virginia.

FURZE *(Ulex europaeus)*. A low, twiggy and spiny shrub, leafless most of the time, never more than 3 feet high. Flowers pea-like, yellow, spring-blooming, but often lasting into July.

Chapter Three

Fragrant Annuals and Perennials

Although permanent fragrance in the garden must always come from the plants in the chapter just ended, perfume in quantity is best secured by growing the ones discussed in this chapter. From them, except the jasmine and rose, most natural perfumes are extracted, and it is these that make parts of southern France, Italy, and Bulgaria a veritable garden of fragrance. As we shall see in another chapter the professionals have various ways of extracting these intoxicating or elusive perfumes, and some of these methods are applicable to the home perfumer. What they all need is an abundance of fresh flowers, and it is from annuals and perennials that we must get them.

And *abundance* means just that. The perfume of plants

comes, in most cases, from an aromatic oil secreted in the petals, ovaries, or nectaries of the flower, usually in almost microscopic amounts, and released a bit at a time so that the flower will be its most ravishing during the whole period of its sexual activity. This may be from a few hours to a week, depending on many factors. It is obvious, then, if we want fragrance in the house, or wish to preserve it in home-made perfume, sachet, or potpourri, we must have a constant supply of fresh flowers at the time when they are at the peak of their fragrance.

The approximate quantities needed will be found in Chapters Six and Seven, and to these must be added those wanted for cutting. The house can be kept constantly perfumed if you plan for it, but again it means growing the annuals and perennials in some quantity. If there is no room in beds or borders, a practical solution is to grow them in rows in the vegetable garden.

Most gardeners will prefer to choose the type of fragrance they want, as was explained in Chapter One, and exemplified in the arrangement of the shrubs and trees in Chapter Two. This, however, is not quite possible in all the herbaceous plants, for many quite fragrant flowers do not conform to any of the six types of fragrance. Some, also, have altogether eluded analysis, and we must fall back on that most important of our organs—the nose. It is the one perfect criterion of fragrance, and it has passed quite critically on the claims of these ten plants.

THE FRAGRANT BUT UNCLASSIFIED TEN

Five of these are annuals, or can be grown as such, and hence one has the opportunity to start as many as the household will need. All except the last one can be sown where wanted.

SWEET PEA. Although all sweet peas are relatively fragrant, the best and most characteristically honey-scented are, among the *purples,* Royal Purple and Perfection; *blues,* Blue Butterfly and Heavenly Blue; *crimsons,* Charity and Unwin's Crimson; *rose-pink,* Empire and Miss Philadelphia. No white varieties are outstandingly fragrant.

SWEET SULTAN. A biennial, but it flowers the first year from seed. Not over 2 feet high, with much cut leaves and a showy head of beautifully musk-scented flowers in midsummer. They may be yellow, red, purple, pink or white.

SWEET ALYSSUM. A popular edging plant, scarcely 8 inches high, the white flowers smelling delightfully of new-mown hay (from coumarin, see Section 1 of Chapter Two). The fragrance is heaviest just after a rain, or in the early morning of heavy dew.

BLISTER CRESS *(Erysimum murale).* 12-18 inches high and leafy. Flowers resembling stocks, golden yellow and with the heavy, sweet odor of orange blossoms.

SWEET SCABIOUS. A tender annual, 2-3 feet high. Flowers in a terminal head, in midsummer, honey-scented. Do not use the many double-flowered varieties. Start seeds in the house and do not plant outdoors until settled warm weather.

Three of these unclassified fragrant plants are very old and favorite perennials, some grown for centuries. All are easily available from dealers in perennial plants.

WALLFLOWER. An ideal plant for the rock wall, as it does not like wet and slushy soil. It grows about one foot high, and bears yellow or orange-brown flowers in early spring of a delicate fragrance. Much grown for cut flowers.

MUSK MALLOW *(Malva moschata)*. 1-2 feet high, the pink flowers of midsummer strongly suggesting the musk used in perfumery. Better and more showy mallows will be found in some related plants, but none with this exotic scent.

RED VALERIAN *(Centranthus ruber)*. A bushy herb, 1-3 feet high with a dense cluster of red flowers in June-July, the odor of which suggests a mixture of honey and lemon.

To provide fragrance both early and late are two bulbous plants among the unclassified ten. Bulbs for the first must be planted the fall before bloom is expected, while the bulbs of the second should be planted in August for bloom the same autumn.

GRAPE HYACINTH. Very early-blooming bulbous plants the small, bell-shaped blue flowers heavily scented with a fruity and musky odor. Plant in masses (100-200) for fine, fragrant carpeting effect.

WINTER DAFFODIL *(Sternbergia lutea)*. A crocus-like plant with yellow, very fragrant flowers that bloom in late autumn, after most autumn crocuses are past. Plant in August about 4 inches deep for bloom in the autumn. They are perfectly hardy as far north as New York.

All the rest of the annuals and perennials appear to lend themselves to their selection for the *types* of fragrance that the grower desires. Before making a choice he, and especially she, is strongly urged to reread most of Chapter One and parts of Chapter Two. For fragrance can be alluring, or contemplative, charming or titillating, romantic or passionate, according to one's mood. And to judge by the literature, some types of fragrance are so close to being an aphrodisiac that perhaps only science would deny it. Two thousand years before Galsworthy wrote *The Dark Flower,* Roman girls were quietly drifting into perdition, not from the comparative innocence of Galsworthy's dark flower (a clove carnation), but from the haunting sex-charged fragrance of musk, ambergris, and many of the flowers found below. This is especially true of those contained in Groups 2 and 3.

Some will say: "Why bother to grow such plants when I can get the same effects from a bottle of perfume, with no effort?" The answer, of course, is that you cannot get the same effects, for perfumery is an art and, however skillful, can never approach the alchemy of nature. Nor can you make a garden of fragrance out of chemical formulas. It takes patience, love, and a little knowledge to plan for a garden of fragrance, especially if you use annuals or perennials in any quantity. Then, too, one must decide *when* fragrance is most desired. If at night, consult the list in Chapter Four. If daytime fragrance is the chief object, the plants below are the varieties to choose, and the month when they bloom is given for guidance.

Arranged according to their *types* of fragrance all the rest of the plants in this chapter can be selected or rejected with the knowledge that they will reflect the temperament of the gardener, and the mood you wish to evoke in your friends.

1. AMINOID—TYPE FLOWER, HAWTHORN

While some mistrust the scent of hawthorn (see Chapter Two) most people like it, and many are charmed with the closely related odor of apple blossoms, the pear, and some species of spirea. The scent, however, is found in only a very few annual and perennial plants. Among them are tulips and scilla.

TULIPS. It must be admitted that the finest of all the tulips, the giant Darwins, are all but scentless. However, especially if cut and brought into a warm room, there is much to be said for Cherry Blossom, Joan of Arc, and Pride of Haarlem, all May flowering.

Among the Cottage Tulips there are several that should be in any fragrant garden, notably Dido, Rosabella, Ellen Willmott, and Arethusa. These, particularly indoors, suggest the delicious scent of some tea roses.

In the Early Tulips some are notably fragrant, but usually more so after being cut than in the open. A good choice might include De Wet, Peach Blossom, and Mrs. Van de Hoeff.

There are, of course, hundreds of other varieties of tulips to be found in the catalogs, but most of them are scentless. One cultivates them mostly for their beauty and color, for as that eminent old Dutch bulb grower, Henry van Oosten, wrote in 1703, "Smell gives them no beauty." However, there are at least ten fragrant tulip varieties, although none of them has a strong or sweet odor.

SCILLA. Smelling strongly of hawthorn, but blooming perhaps a fortnight earlier, is the bluebells of England (*Scilla nonscripta*). A low, bulbous plant, very beautiful if planted by the hundreds, it has a delightful, but not strong scent. Meadows at Kew are blue with it. There are pink and white flowered varieties, but for fragrance it is better to select the common blue sort.

PASSION FLOWER *(Passiflora caerulea).* A Brazilian vine, with extraordinary pink flowers nearly 4 inches wide, but with a crown of white and purple. Its fancied resemblance to the Crucifixion so impressed the first Spaniards who saw it that it become a symbol of the ordeal on the Cross, a significance it still holds for many. Its odor resembles the hawthorn, but unfortunately it is not quite hardy north of Washington, D. C., and even precarious there. However, if killed to the ground it usually sends up new growth the following spring. Do not attempt it north of Washington.

2. HEAVY—TYPE FLOWER, JASMINE

(See also Chapter One and Section 2 of Chapter Two)

Judith may have been a jade, but she knew what she was about when she took off to seduce Holofernes, for she "anointed herself with precious ointment, and decked herself bravely, to allure the eyes of all men that should see her." So it reads in the *Book of Judith,* but ever since, and long before, women have understood the lure of fragrance, used it shamelessly or transmuted its indefinable charm into poetry, art, music, or the refinements of feminine coquetry that always tame the male, however crass.

Among annuals and perennials, there are not many that can properly be classed among these *Heavy* and frankly seductive odors, but there are several among the *Aromatic* section which come close to the plants that were in the "precious ointment" of Judith. No gardener should plant these in quantities, near the house, or porch, or patio without realizing that many of them, in spite of exquisite fragrance, have a past steeped in sin. By far the most important is:

THE TUBEROSE

Shelley called it "The daintiest flower for scent that blows," but in India it was, perhaps more realistically, called "Mistress of the Night." Although its odor, particularly in our climate, is perfectly obvious during the daytime, in hot climates its fragrance is enhanced by dusk and becomes intoxicating with darkness. It should perhaps, on this account, have been put among the night-scented flowers in Chapter Four, but it is *the* perfume plant of France, or perhaps second only to the jasmine and the rose. It is certainly more seductive than the latter. With the jasmine it comprises the two most fragrant plants in this book.

Unlike the jasmine, whose culture is restricted in this country by climatic requirements (see Chapter Two, Section 2), the tuberose can be grown anywhere if the autumn months are not afflicted with too early frosts. A native of Mexico, it is not permanently hardy outdoors throughout the country, so that its culture is very like that of gladiolus. In other words, the bulbs cannot be planted until all danger of frost is passed and must be lifted before really cold weather. It sends up long, basal leaves, followed by a white, waxy-petalled flower of such incredibly sweet fragrance, in late September and October, that it is all but overpowering. The offsets found when the bulb is dug for winter storage, will not flower the next season, so that if blooms are wanted every year it is better to purchase flowering bulbs each spring. Thousands of acres of it are grown in southern France for perfume.

Quite unrelated to the tuberose, but with a fragrance almost as sweet, is the delicate little lily-of-the-valley which is perfectly hardy and can be grown anywhere in partial or deep shade. Be sure to get the ordinary, single-flowered, white variety, not a double-flowered or pink sort. In early May the beautiful, bell-shaped flowers, much favored for bouquets, are profuse in small clusters. Keats called it "the sweet Lily of the lovely vale," and poets ever since have sung its praises. Once established the plant will make large patches.

Most of the rest of the heavy-scented flowers come from bulbous plants and hence are easily grown, but one of our native woody herbs warrants a place in any fragrant garden—but only if the gardener will provide the specialized conditions it demands. This is the beautiful trailing arbutus or Mayflower, which produces its very sweet-smelling, rather small, white or pinkish flowers in late March or April, depending on its site. It grows naturally in sandy or rocky woods, needs an acid soil, and should be purchased as a potted plant from dealers who specialize in native wild flowers. Few native plants are so sweet-scented as trailing arbutus, but it will not grow in ordinary garden soil. Once established in the right kind of site it will grow and spread—but slowly for it is a shy beauty.

HEAVY-SCENTED BULBOUS PLANTS

The two groups below are easily grown in any ordinary garden soils. Among many relatives in each group, of indifferent odor or none, they have been selected for their outstanding fragrance. In both narcissus and lilies, because of the failure of related species to have any appreciable odor or to have an actually repulsive one, it is important to order them by the names given below. All are perfectly hardy.

LILIES. There are many species and varieties of these gorgeous flowers in cultivation and some authorities credit all of them with fragrance. It may be true under certain conditions, but the average gardener has room only for a small selection and the following five have been chosen because of their undisputed fragrance. All bloom in summer, and their fragrance has been called "brooding and sultry." Other lilies are so stinking that one expert exclaimed, "May dogs devour its hateful bulbs."

MADONNA LILY. *(Lilium candidum).* 3-4 feet. Flowers white, waxy and nearly 3 inches long.

WHITE-TRUMPET LILY *(Lilium longiflorum).* 2-3 feet. Flowers trumpet-shaped, pure white, nearly 7 inches long. It is related to the Easter Lily.

LILIUM AURATUM. 4-6 feet, and without a common name, although much cultivated. Flowers nearly 10 inches long, white, but crimson-spotted and with a central yellow band.

ROYAL LILY *(Lilium regale).* 4-5 feet. Flowers about 6 inches long, lilac-purple outside, but yellow at the base and white inside.

JAPANESE LILY *(Lilium speciosum).* 3-4 feet. Flowers about 4 inches long, white or pale pink, rose-spotted. Its scent is too heavily sweet to be liked by all.

NARCISSUS. Most of the common yellow, trumpet narcissus varieties are without enough odor to be worth cultivating for that object. But besides the paper-white narcissus, and its equally fragrant relative the so-called Chinese Sacred Lily, neither of which can be grown outdoors, there are two hardy species of outstanding fragrance.

JONQUIL *(Narcissus jonquilla)*. 12-18 inches high. Flowers yellow, about 1 inch long. Do not take double-flowered or color variants.

POET'S NARCISSUS *(Narcissus poeticus)*. 12-18 inches high. Flowers white, extremely fragrant, not more than 1 inch long. It is safer to avoid double-flowered varieties, or those of any variety other than the typical form.

3. AROMATIC—TYPE FLOWER, CLOVE PINK

(See, also Chapter Two, Section 3)

Many of the flowers in this group could almost as well be classed among the heavily scented plants just discussed; for the aromatics *are* heavily scented, but they have, most of them, a distinctly spicy odor. They are less sultry, seductive, and have fewer sex-linked connotations than cling to jasmine, the tuberose, and those wicked scents of which the debauched Romans were so fond.

On the other hand, no one should dismiss the *Aromatics* as flowers without a past. Such a discriminating gardener as John Galsworthy wove one of his hauntingly beautiful stories around one of them, *The Dark Flower*. And for anyone who reads it, the fragrance of the clove carnation will forever stir a pang for Mark and his pursuit of the unattainable.

One of the completely inexplicable things about fragrance, which baffles all the sciences, is the capacity of odors to bring back memories, clearly and instantly, of things in the past. It may be years ago or it may have happened only yesterday, but a particular scent will bring it back, when mere memory has buried it under layers of other things. It is precisely in this capacity that the *Aromatic* group excel all others, perhaps because of the complexity of the compounds that are chiefly responsible for their fragrance (see Chapter One).

Here, fortunately for the gardener, are many old favorites besides the clove pink or carnation and its relatives, the hyacinth, primrose, stocks, a couple of annuals, and some perennials.

CARNATIONS AND PINKS

"Quaint, gay, sweet and good for nosegays"

When Linnaeus created the genus *Dianthus,* he quite properly included the carnation, all the known pinks, and what were for a century or so known as gilliflowers, a name now nearly obsolete. For the carnation he coined the name *Dianthus caryophyllus,* the latter finally being distilled through the French *giroflee* into our English *Gilliflower.* What matters more than this etymological excursion is that the wise, old Linnaeus called the carnation *caryophyllus* because that was the Latin name for the clove, and as he well knew there is scarcely one of the whole tribe that does not have the rich, spicy odor we know so well in our modern carnation.

All of the original species of *Dianthus* were single-flowered plants with five petals, but the florists and gardeners have developed the multi-petalled forms we see today and incidentally raised the fragrance to a degree of intensity unknown in their wild ancestors.

For the gardener seeking fragrance today it is well to remember that *Dianthus* is a genus of almost 200 species. A selection of them is all that anyone, however enthusiastic over their fragrance, can possibly grow, remembering that of the carnation itself there are over a hundred named forms—some of them grown by the millions by the florists. A reasonable selection might hence include:

CARNATION *(Dianthus caryophyllus)*. This, which is also known as the clove pink, cannot be grown continuously outdoors over most of the country, if one is considering only the florist's flower to which the name "carnation" is usually applied.

But there are strains or varieties of it that are reasonably hardy in the south and can be grown outdoors if one can give them a bit of protection over the winter. None of them is as fragrant as the florist's carnation, but they make a very agreeable substitute for it. They are much more commonly grown in England than here, for that island has a better climate for them than ours. Among the varieties of these hardy carnations, the deep red or crimson sorts are the most fragrant.

GRASS PINK *(Dianthus plumarius)*. A perfectly hardy, mat-forming perennial, 9-18 inches high, with bluish-gray foliage and single rose-pink flowers (white in some varieties) with fringed petals. May.

CHEDDAR PINK *(Dianthus caesius)*. A turf-forming perennial, 3-9 inches high, its matted foliage bluish-green. Flowers rose-red, about 1½ inches wide, with fringed petals. May.

There are several other fragrant species of *Dianthus,* but the Sweet William *(Dianthus barbatus)* is all but scentless.

STOCKS

Perhaps the most fragrant of all stocks is the night-scented or evening stock, which withholds its delicious scent until nightfall and hence is to be found in the chapter devoted to nocturnal fragrance (Chapter Four). Among the day-flowering sort, however, there are several varieties of such sweet, spicy odor that they, too, were once called Gillyflower, because their fragrance is carnation-like. Among them is the Brompton stock, named for a suburb of London, which is a perennial that is inclined to die out in a couple of years. Much more common are the Ten-week stocks which are annuals and have spikes of showy flowers, the blooming of which can be prolonged by sowing a succession of seed. For the earliest lot, start in a cold frame, hotbed, or in a box in the kitchen window, 14 weeks before bloom is wanted. Select a single-flowered variety for best fragrance, although some of the more showy, double-flowered sorts are also acceptable.

It should be remembered that nearly all stocks are predominately spicy or aromatic in their fragrance, but they also contain a tinge, and some think a dangerous tinge, of the heavy odors of the plants in Section 2 of this chapter. So penetrating is the scent that half a dozen sprays will completely dominate the fragrance of a room.

HYACINTH AND CROCUS

Both these bulbous groups contain heavily spiced fragrance, especially the hyacinth, which, besides its balsam-like odor, has a nearly sovereign sweetness, which to some is a bit overpowering. Bulbs of these early-blooming hyacinths should be planted in late October or November for bloom the following May. All of the horticultural varieties are supremely fragrant, and from more than 200 named forms known to be in cultivation here, yellow, blue, white, pink, and deep red sorts can be selected with confidence that they will be fragrant.

Crocus. Practically none of the low, common, spring-flowering varieties of crocus have any odor worth mentioning, but one spring-flowering species and two autumn-blooming sorts are decidedly fragrant. To distinguish them from the common, scentless varieties, the more favored ones are best ordered by their Latin names. The spring-flowering ones should be planted in the fall, while the autumn-blooming kind needs August planting for bloom in October. These are not the usual autumn crocus, which belong to *Colchicum* and are practically scentless.

Crocus imperati, spring-flowering, the flowers lilac or white, with the scent of cowslip.

Crocus longiflorus, autumn-flowering, the lilac flower with a bearded yellow throat and primrose-scented.

Crocus sativus, often called Saffron crocus or vegetable gold. An autumn-flowering crocus with white or lilac-purple flowers having yellow, aromatic stigmas from which commercial saffron is derived in southern Europe where it is grown for the purpose.

THREE AROMATIC PERENNIALS

The lavender, primrose, and our shooting star are the only common garden perennials that are easily available and can be properly put among the *Aromatics.* Not one of them has a tinge of the heavy odor of hyacinth, nor, of course, of the tuberose or jasmine. Each of them is grown for a certain spicy or aromatic scent which is enticing and lively, but has no whiff of seduction about it.

LAVENDER. An old garden favorite grown chiefly for its fragrant foliage which is ashy-gray. The flowers, however, which are lavender-purple, have the same delightful fragrance that is derived from the foliage for making lavender water. Dried flowers retain their odor for months, which is why girls since the days of the Romans like to sprinkle it among their clothes. It is really a low shrub.

PRIMROSES. It is unfortunate that most of the species in the genus *Primula* require moist and especially shady or half-shady sites. It is generally useless to try them in full sun, for they do not like summer heat or dryness. If you have the right conditions all of the following can be grown, and they are delightfully fragrant. All are spring-blooming.

PRIMROSE *(Primula vulgaris).* 3-6 inches high, the flowers yellow. This is *the* primrose of English song and story, which the poets from Spenser to Keats have immortalized. There are today many horticultural varieties, but the common, old-fashioned sort is the safest to use for fragrance.

COWSLIP *(Primula veris).* 4-8 inches high, the yellow flowers with an orange eye. Many varieties are known; some are double-flowered, but are best avoided for surety of fragrance. Like most of the primroses there is a whiff of anise in its scent.

AURICULA *(Primula auricula).* 5-8 inches high, the flowers variously colored, but always with an eye. Among acceptable varieties are Double Red, Rosebud, Scarlet Prince, and White Ensign.

Shooting Star *(Dodecatheon meadia)*. A beautiful, native wild flower, 8-12 inches high, its delicate mauve-pink flowers appearing in late May or June, spicy with a cinnamon-like odor. It prefers partial shade.

TWO AROMATIC ANNUALS

The common garden heliotrope and the sand verbena share alike in their delightful almond, or almond plus vanilla, odor, the quantity of which is limited only by how many you grow. Both provide a delicious perfume for a room, while in the case of heliotrope there is also a whiff of the heavy scent of those plants in Section 2 of this chapter.

Heliotrope. This is really a perennial, but because it is likely to die out it is best grown as an annual and, for the greatest fragrance, always in the greenhouse. Lacking that, start seed in the cold frame, hotbed, or in the kitchen window in March, transplanting outdoors when settled warm weather has arrived. They will bloom the first season from seedlings so started.

Sand Verbena *(Abronia umbellata)*. The verbena-like flower of this prostrate, vine-like plant develops its pink bloom in June. It, like the heliotrope, is really a perennial, but best treated as a tender annual. Plant seeds indoors in March.

4. VIOLET—TYPE FLOWER, THE FLORIST'S VIOLET

Not many flowers have the scent of violets, and only a handful of violets themselves have it, for nearly all the American wild kinds are practically scentless. Even the delightful odor of the florist's violet is little more than a wistful will-o'-the-wisp, fading all too swiftly as only a memory. Also, the flower is not one for the general amateur, for it will not grow outdoors over most of the country and hence needs a cool greenhouse or a hotbed.

The horned violet or tufted pansy, while perfectly hardy, is not worth cultivating for fragrance, so that the average home grower, without a hotbed or greenhouse, may well ask himself, is it impossible to produce the wonderful odor of the florist's violet in my garden?

There is a solution to this apparent impasse only because *Viola odorata* comes in many forms. By far the most fragrant are the double-flowered varieties, bred for odor and for growing under glass by professionals. These are not for the amateur. But some other forms of *Viola odorata* can be grown outdoors. One of them is a variety of the Neapolitan violet known as Marie Louise, which has double-flowered, beautifully fragrant, reddish-purple bloom. Also, some single-flowered forms of *Viola odorata* are available from specialists, but if the truth must out, the violet fragrance so well known in Europe is not easily obtainable here—at least in the average outdoor garden.

All the more welcome then is the beloved Egyptian weed, with a violet-like odor, which charmed Paris so much that they called it immediately *mignonette* (little darling), a name that has pushed into the background not only its Latin cognomen of *Reseda odorata* but a dozen others.

When it first reached Paris, about the middle of the eighteenth century, the ease of its culture soon filled every window box, and a year or two later London went as mad as that staid city ever becomes over the enchanting odor of the newcomer which they thought was a French flower. London markets were soon packed with it, and our gardens have been ever since. It can be grown anywhere, for it is an annual of the easiest culture. Only a few plants will scent up a whole garden, but it is not for cutting, for once out of the sun it loses its odor rather quickly. As in so many other fragrant plants, it is safer to get true *Reseda odorata,* and not some of the fancy, modern varieties the odor of which has been almost bred out of them.

This odor of violets is such a comparatively rare occurrence in the plant world (it is found in some tropical trees) that two widely different bulbous plants that have it are nearly as welcome as the mignonette. They are:

MEXICAN STAR *(Milla biflora).* A bulbous plant with grass-like leaves and a stalk 12-18 inches high, at the end of which is a beautifully fragrant white flower about 2½ inches wide. Blooms in midsummer and is to be grown exactly as gladiolus.

SNOWFLAKE *(Leucojum vernum).* Whoever named the snowflake *Leucojum* (that is, a white violet) must have smelled the violet-like odor of these beautiful, spring-flowering bulbs. As the name indicates, they are among our first flowers to bloom after snow has gone. Plant in fall for next spring's bloom, and once started they persist for many years.

5. ROSE—TYPE FLOWER, THE FRAGRANT ROSES

(See Section 5 of Chapter Two)

Scarcely any perennials or annuals have the true "rose scent," and as we have seen, not many modern roses have it. But the fragrance of roses, or something very like it, is found among certain irises and in a few peonies.

IRIS

Most modern iris varieties are scentless or nearly so, but *Iris reticulata,* a very early blooming species has a combination of odors including whiffs of violet and rose. It is perhaps the most fragrant of all cultivated irises.

Some enthusiasts, who are a little more ecstatic than factual, would have it that *all* irises are fragrant. Many have a faint odor, but this book is dedicated to providing the amateur gardener with varieties that are fragrant enough to give some compelling reason for cultivating them.

Among thousands of iris varieties generally grouped as tall bearded or German iris, there are a few notably fragrant. These are likely to contain some trace of the blood of *Iris pallida,* a wild species with a delicious odor of vanilla, civet, violet, and rose. Such a combination is as complicated as the genetic history of most horticultural varieties of iris. The following ten seem worth cultivation, considering only their fragrance:

- Afterglow
- Aphrodite
- Frieda Mohr
- Mandalay
- Mary Barnett
- Morning Splendor
- Queen Caterina
- Sir Galahad
- Souvenir de Mme. Gaudichau
- Zua

PEONY

Many peonies, in spite of their spectacular flower, are all but scentless, and some are downright repulsive. Even among the fragrant sorts listed below, all of which have a tinge of rose scent in them, none is outstandingly fragrant. They are mentioned here because everyone wants to grow these magnificent perennials, and to choose at least a few fragrant varieties seems essential.

Avalanche	John M. Good	Kelway's Queen
Duchess de Nemours	Katherine Havemyer	Lamartine
Frances Shaylor	Nell Shaylor	Marie Lemoine
Jesse Shaylor		

6. LEMON—TYPE FLOWER, FOUR-O'CLOCK

(See Chapter One, and Section 6 of Chapter Two)

No flowers have the characteristic odor found in the rind of the lemon and some other citrus fruits, but some have a fragrance that suggests this highly aromatic odor, because they contain citral, a compound chiefly responsible for the scent of that pungent oil found in most lemon rinds, especially those from Italy. This lemon-like fragrance is found among some magnolias and other trees and shrubs discussed in Chapter Two, but in only a handful of herbaceous plants. Of these the annual and somewhat weedy four-o'clock is paramount, followed by our exquisite native water lily and a prairie evening primrose, which because it is chiefly night-blooming is noted in the next chapter.

FOUR-O'CLOCK. This is a perennial in its native South America, where it is often known as Marvel-of-Peru, and it may often be perennial in our South. But in the North it is best treated as a tender annual, since it blooms the same season from seed if these are sown early in March in boxes set in the kitchen window. The preference in this book for kitchen windows does not mean that the living room is no place for plants. But the kitchen is a work room; hence it is cooler and usually moister than any living room, especially from the evaporation from sinks and the steam from cooking. Kitchen windows, therefore, are ideal places to start seedlings.

The four-o'clock, which can be set outdoors as soon as warm weather is assured, is rather weedy, 14-30 inches high, and will bloom all summer, especially under partial shade, where it blooms all day. Its name suggests the fact that in open sunlight it really opens its typically reddish flowers only as the light begins to fade. Varieties of it come also in white and yellow shades, but the old-fashioned red sort is to be preferred for fragrance, which is a delicate combination of lemon and fruit scents.

WATER LILY *(Nymphaea odorata)*. This beautiful, white-flowered floating aquatic cannot, of course, be grown unless you have a pool or can sink a half-barrel in the lawn. It is one of the most delightfully fragrant of all the native plants in the eastern United States. The odor is lemony, but mixed with it there are spicy or aromatic elements that make it quite entrancing. Be sure to order by the Latin name for many of its relatives and even some of its derivative varieties are practically scentless.

Chapter Four

Night Witchery

The Romans, Persians, and Arabs understood the arts of perfumery better than any of us, and they used flowers on such a scale that no rich prodigal of today would dream of like extravagance. Before carpets became general, it was not unusual for a prince to strew with rose petals the floor of a banquet room to the depth of a wine glass.

When the strict and puritanical Christians frowned on perfumes, as well they might considering what had been done with them, the more tolerant *Koran* encouraged perfumes and especially the growing of the flowers that were then the only source of these intoxicating essences.

While the drab Christians of the Middle Ages were plodding a scentless path to the Renaissance, except for incense in the

Church, the far more civilized Arabs and Persians were exploring every avenue of sensuous enjoyment. From prince to pauper the love of flowers was a passion, and none knew better than they the far greater impact of fragrance as daylight wanes and dusk turns to darkness. To the witchery of night they added the noctural lure of flowers that are scentless by day but, as one poet has said:

> All night incense's sweetest fragrance
> Rises from those perfumed bowers,
> Through the moonlight's silver radiance
> From the yellow jasmine flowers.

Nature, too, seems in league with gardeners who want to capture the enchantment of night fragrance. For then the dusty heat of day is followed by the cool air of evening, and one by one the flowers that were either closed or scentless during sunshine steal into our consciousness, not only by their odor but by their color.

Many night-blooming plants have white flowers, and such an observant poet as Tennyson recorded the sequence of flower visibility as night falls.

> Now sleeps the crimson petal, now the white

It is no accident that among these white-flowered, nocturnal blooms are some of the most intoxicating odors known to the seeker of fragrance. This startling whiteness, amid the gloom of night, is one of nature's tricks to guide night-flying moths, so that the nuptials of these fragrant flowers of the dusk may be completed when they are most receptive. There is an extraordinary correlation between the incidence of these night-flying moths and the white floral virgins of the night waiting for a ghostly visitor who will complete their love life.

There is far more to this than the poetic imagery of flower and insect—for it ultimately involves the survival of both. We need not here go into the fascinating by-paths of the marvellously timed operations implied by the nocturnal darting of perfumed moths among perfumed and nocturnal flowers. No one, however, can escape the implications of an atmosphere redolent with the fragrance of sex.

It is precisely this which was so well known to the ancients. And it should be thoroughly understood by any modern gardener who wants either to avoid the perils or to promote the potentialities of night fragrance in the garden. Which you choose will dictate what flowers you select from those mentioned below. Some are as fragrant as any others in this book. Some belong to the "dangerous" scents that the susceptible must use with caution. These are among Groups 2 and 3 of the *types* of fragrance that have been noted in Chapter One and need not be repeated here. To make selection easier each of the plants below, if it is known, will carry a number enclosed in brackets thus: [2], [3], etc. This, of course, means that such plants belong to the same *types* of fragrance as those detailed in the first chapter.

It is urged that before planning a night garden of fragrance, or even planting a few of the species in an existing garden, the reader scan that chapter with this in mind:

Must your night garden of fragrance reflect the mature scents of the middle-aged or do you want it to be a thing of haunting beauty, sex-charged with the mystery of night and perfumed with the intoxicating fragrance which drove Sappho in her ode to Aphrodite to write (about 600 B.C.)

Its beauties charm the gods above;
Its fragrance is the breath of Love;
Its foliage wantons in the air;
Luxuriant, like the flowing hair.

If hair is no longer flowing, the lady who wrote that shares with her cropped and curled sister of today the universal knowledge that fragrance lures by day but bewitches by night.

PLANT MATERIALS FOR THE NIGHT-FRAGRANT GARDEN

Scarcely anyone would inflict upon themselves or their guests a garden devoted wholly to nocturnal flowers. The desire to have some near an open window, a porch, in a patio, or in some quiet nook in the garden must dictate what sort of fragrance you want, when it will be available, and if it is to be a shrub, vine, or a perennial or annual herb.

The materials are not copious, for in spite of all the poets the number of plants that both bloom and are fragrant at night is rather limited. This is especially true if one excludes all tropical sorts such as the fabulous Queen-of-the-Night, of which one poet wrote that she

. . . bares her breast
Of fragrant scent, a virgin white,
A pearl amidst the realms of night.

There appear to be no trees with night-fragrant flowers, and among shrubs the honeysuckles are the most likely, and they are among the most heavily scented of all shrubs. Two of them are really both day and night fragrant, or at least the odor from both of them is greater after dark. One is a rather low shrub

(Lonicera heckrotti) [3]* of unknown origin and without a common name, but of exquisite fragrance. The other is the Old World woodbine *(Lonicera periclymenum)* [3], a scrambling vine up to 20 feet high, with yellowish-white, but red-tinged flowers that bloom most of the summer. For other honeysuckles, all day-blooming, see Chapter Two.

Much less disturbing (for honeysuckles are notoriously that) is a stout woody vine, with the odor of magnolia, but having rather inconspicuous flowers, known as *Akebia quinata* [6], a description of which will be found in Section 6 of Chapter Two.

If this seems a meagre list of night fragrant shrubs and vines the gardener should not forget that Nature has been much more prolific with them in tropical and sub-tropical lands. Scarcely any of these can be grown here and one must hence leave for more favored gardeners the rich odors of the night that come from many orchids, from the orange blossom, and scores of tropical shrubs and trees like the frangipani and ylang-ylang.

NIGHT-FRAGRANT ANNUALS AND PERENNIALS

It is from these, of course, that evening scents must come *en masse,* particularly in the case of annuals. These can be sown in any quantity, moved from year to year and provide not only fragrance in the garden but serve as a steady supply for the house.

Before discussing either group it is well to remind the reader

* The numbers in brackets refer to the types of fragrance as detailed in Chapter One. They are important for those who want something more than just any kind of fragrance.

that some plants, noted in Chapters Two and Three, are also night-fragrant, particularly in the warmer sections of the country. Of these, two are probably the most fragrant plants in the temperate world—the jasmine and tuberose. Hence, in planning for night fragrance these should not be ignored for they are more fragrant and far more bewitching than the plants below, although some of the annuals have driven poets and gardeners to the verge of speechlessness!

ANNUALS

All of the seven plants grouped as annuals are not true annuals, but are best treated as such. Some are tender annuals which should be started in the greenhouse, hotbed, or in boxes in the kitchen window. Some are biennials and hence need constant renewal. One or two are short-lived perennials (sometimes permanent in warm sections of the country), but, for continuance of supply, they are best treated by the constant renewal of annual seed planting.

NIGHT PHLOX *(Zaluzianskya villosa)*. A tender annual from South Africa, scarcely 12 inches high, related to snapdragon, but exquisitely night-fragrant from its purplish flowers that are white or pale lilac on the inside. The seed is sometimes, but incorrectly, offered as *Nycterinia selaginoides,* but under whatever name the plant demands a place in any garden of night fragrance.

Nicotiana [3] and [2]. When Columbus first saw the Indians in Cuba smoking tobacco in November 1492, he little realized that tobacco would capture the world, and a relative of it equally capture the affections of all gardeners who seek night fragrance. For besides *Nicotiana tabacum,* there are several annual species, of no use for making tobacco, but some of them having flowers that are among the most fragrant ever to scent the night air.

Of these by far the best is *Nicotiana alata grandiflora* [3] and [2], which is really a perennial from Brazil, Uruguay, and Paraguay and is so extraordinarily fragrant that it is often called Jasmine Tobacco. It sometimes seeds itself, but is best treated as a tender annual. It will grow up to 3-4 feet, with long, tubular white flowers that are usually closed (open in the shade) all day, but which expand in the evening and give off an intoxicating scent. There is a related species, *Nicotiana sylvestris* [3] and [2], which is a true perennial, and has a slightly less enticing fragrance.

Night-scented Stock. *(Mathiola bicornis)* [3] and [2]. Often called the evening stock, this annual or biennial herb from the Old World is nothing to rave about by day, for its small, brown-purple flowers are shut tight until sundown. Then they open and give off such a fragrance that if a single cluster is brought into the house it will scent up a whole room. For a succession of its enticing fragrance it is well to make small sowings every ten days up to the middle of July.

Evening Campion *(Lychnis alba)* [2]. An almost weedy roadside herb, naturalized here from Europe. It is not common in usual gardens, for not enough people know about its almost jasmine-like night fragrance. Actually it is a biennial which seeds itself along roadsides and ditches, but can easily be started in the garden from purchased seeds. It is a sticky herb, 1-2 feet high, its white flowers fringed, summer-blooming.

DAME'S ROCKET *(Hesperis matronalis)* [3]. This biennial often called double white rocket, came originally from Europe and Asia, but has been popular in England for centuries. It is a branching plant, 2-3 feet high, the flowers white, purple or lilac, quite open by day, but giving off its spicy fragrance only at night.

SCHIZOPETALON WALKERI [3]. A beautifully night-fragrant Chilean annual, rather sprawling in habit and never over 12 inches high. Its white flowers, which are handsomely fringed and borne in terminal clusters, have an extraordinary odor at night—sweet, but compounded of almond and vanilla. The seed is best sown where wanted, for the plant does not like transplanting, but they should not be started outdoors until settled warm weather.

PRAIRIE LILY *(Mentzelia decapetala)*. This very showy prairie biennial, native from South Dakota to Texas is not well known to Eastern gardeners, but it should be since seeds are available from dealers in prairie wild flowers. It is scarcely a foot high and has white or yellow flowers nearly 5 inches wide, the petals velvet-like. Sow the seeds where wanted and it may persist from self-sown seeds.

PERENNIALS

Only four garden perennials are both night-blooming and night-fragrant, and even one of these is perennial only in the South. Others could no doubt be found, and some of them have adherents, but they are omitted here because of their difficult cultivation or their unavailability to all but the specialists.

One of them has the not inappropriate specific name *tristis,* which technically means sad, bitter, or dull; or, by extension, that they are not much to look at by day. But at night how different the story! Shy, sad, and dull by day, but like some ladies, they put on the raiment of charm as the sun goes down.

In Chapter Three there is an omission that may have struck the gardener. Why omit the gorgeous and multi-named varieties of gladiolus? The truth is that practically all of them are scentless, and it is only among the wild species of *Gladiolus* that we can expect real fragrance. Of these, *Gladiolus tristis* [3] from South Africa is not only very fragrant, but does not begin to be so until sundown. It is smaller than the common horticultural varieties and does not have the usual sword-shaped leaves. Flowers are yellowish-white, streaked with purple. It is grown exactly as are its more showy relatives—in other words its corms must be planted each June and lifted over the winter. It would be a hardy perennial in its natural climate.

The remaining night-fragrant perennials are:

Daylily. These lily-like perennials should, from their common name, bloom only by day. All belong to the genus *Hemerocallis* and among them is one species that blooms at night and is deliciously fragrant after dusk. It is *Hemerocallis thunbergi* [2] from Japan, about 2 feet high with lemon-yellow, lily-like flowers about 2-3 inches long which bloom in midsummer. Most daylilies are scentless, except one or two known as lemon lilies, so that this night-fragrant Japanese perennial is a welcome addition to the tribe.

Bouncing Bet *(Saponaria officinalis)* [3]. A decidedly weedy Asiatic immigrant, naturalized everywhere here, and especially fond of the cindery wastes along the railroad. No one would think of growing it in the garden were it not for the wonderful, spicy, carnation-like odor of its flowers, which is obvious only at night. It is a sturdy plant, 1-3 feet high with pinkish-white flowers, and by no means to be despised because is comes from the wrong side of the tracks.

EVENING PRIMROSE *(Oenothera caespitosa)* [6]. From our prairie region come many kinds of evening primroses and their relatives that bloom by day, but nearly all are scentless and some positively repulsive. All the more welcome, then, is this beautiful and, in fact, extremely showy perennial from the prairie states. It is low, has basal leaves, and about sundown it begins to expand a flower that is nearly 4 inches wide, generally white, but tinged with pink. The fragrance is strongly suggestive of some sweet-smelling magnolia.

Chapter Five

Fragrance in the House

No scientist has ever yet been able to plot on a graph the fragrance of flowers or our emotional response to the wildly different *types* of fragrance. We do know something about the intensity of scent—mild in a tulip but ravishing in the jasmine, captivating in the carnation but elusive in the violet, enticing in the mignonette but easily raising quite unholy emotions in the tuberose.

Although scent is just as unmeasurable as our reactions to it, there are a few things we know about flower fragrance that seem warranted by the perfume history of those who have done more than any others to make it an art. It seems clear enough that the *heavy* and *aromatic* (See Chapter One for definitions) types of fragrance were and still are cherished by the Mediterranean, Arabian, Persian, Semitic, and Indian peoples based upon their clear recognition of the fact that the appeal was frankly sensuous and, even more frankly, sexual, especially in fragrance such as jasmine and tuberose. The idea may seem almost repulsive to those who think of fragrance as a symbol of purity. But the evidence points all the other way. Here are the ardent races, passionate and even obsessed by sex, for as one writer has so well put it, "In India the very children are the waifs of sex."

Such people need no graphs to measure fragrance. They know, or think they do, what its significance means. And one of the most scholarly of all writers on flower fragrance has amply confirmed it. He points out, particularly where *heavy* types of fragrance are involved, that these magic flower essences were not created for our enjoyment, but to complete the sex life of the flower and that of the equally perfumed butterflies or moths which pollinate those flowers.

It is, according to F. A. Hampton,* no accident that these sweetly heavy odors unconsciously stir the mating instinct, because we too respond to the very sex-linked factors that have produced that fragrance. Nor is it any accident that from Cleopatra to today all the distilled fragrance of flowers is used by women—if we exclude a coterie of perfumed dandies ancient and modern. Such heavy odors are perhaps not really aphrodisiac but they come close to it, for as Hampton says, "A sweet scent is one that can stir the instinct of courtship without evoking the idea of the natural end object of the

* Hampton, F. A., *The Scent of Flowers and Leaves,* London, Dulau and Co., 1925. See particularly pp. 78-84. The classification of fragrance in this book has been adapted in part from Mr. Hampton's modification of the older scheme of Count Kerner von Marilaun, an Austrian botanist.

instinct." So true is this, and so basic is our response, that it is scarcely surprising that anthropologists have turned up a primitive tribe in Somaliland in which girls smear their bodies with a peculiarly sex-excitant kind of musk extracted from crocodiles.

It is easy to catch the critical chorus of feminine readers who will be saying, "What's all this to do with Fragrance in the House? My house is no harem and I'm not trying to imitate Cleopatra or evoke anything that an imaginative scientist may dream up; all I want is to give pleasure to myself and guests." To these unimpeachable sentiments the answer is so obvious that it scarcely needs laboring. For whether we know it or not, or will admit it at all, fragrance does affect the senses just as poor half-crazed Baudelaire knew when he wrote "My soul hovers over perfumes as the soul of others hovers over music."

Fragrance in the house, just as in the open, can be arranged and planned, depending on our mood and the emotions we wish to evoke. There are, however, a few limitations on bringing flowers indoors which depend upon the plants themselves and especially on the conditions in the garden that will promote or retard fragrance; whether their scent will be available during the day or night; how long it will last; and, particularly, whether an extremely fragrant flower in the garden will lose it if picked at all—such as mignonette and wallflowers.

As to those fit for cutting that are only night-fragrant—the obvious time to gather them is about or just before sundown because their fragrance will last all night, and most of them will close up the next morning. Many of them will be useless the next evening, with a few notable exceptions to be stressed presently.

Fragrance in nearly all plants resides mostly in their petals, and the compounds responsible for the odor are usually rather heavy oils found in microscopic amounts and of greatly varying capacity to rouse our senses. In most day-blooming flowers, stillness and moisture definitely releases more scent than wind and dryness. That is why picking flowers for fragrance is best done in the cool of the morning, while the dew is still on them if possible, or else about sunset. Even more than in non-fragrant flowers, it is important to keep fragrant cut flowers from withering, and a good precaution is to plunge the stems in a bucket of water as they are picked. A cloudy or even a foggy day makes an ideal time for picking because transpiration is much reduced at such periods.

What has been said applies to most plants that you will be growing yourself in the open fragrant garden. It is not always true, however, regarding many greenhouse flowers that are purchased from florists. For some reason, as yet all but unknown, most greenhouse-raised flowers have their fragrance markedly increased by bringing them into a room of ordinary temperature. This is especially true of roses and carnations and is strikingly so in gardenia, freesia, bouvardia, stephanotis, stocks, violets, and greenhouse-forced lily-of-the-valley. Most of these, except roses and violets, belong to the *heavy* or *aromatic* type of fragrance.

But most people with a fragrant garden will want to cut their own supplies, and before listing the most desirable, it is well to decide which rooms are to have them and what sort of atmosphere you wish to create. It is, for instance, almost axiomatic that few fragrant flowers should be in the dining room, and no heavy or aromatic ones at all should ever be put on the dining table for the very good reason that Nature has linked our sense of smell and taste just a bit too closely.

It is a commonplace that, as a head cold increases, our sense of taste fades, but it is not so generally known that if you pinch your nose hard enough you can scarcely "taste" an onion. In other words our sense of taste and smell is compounded of an intricate biological association, far too complicated to be enlarged upon here. The end result, according to some experts, is that, without smell, we can distinguish only a few tastes such as salt, sweet, and sour, especially the puckery taste of gooseberries.

Nearly all other tastes, especially of the things we like the best, are thus not pure "taste" at all, but a blend of taste and smell—in what proportion we can leave to the experts. What it means to the initiated at the dining room table is obvious. Who for instance wants to blend roast beef with bouvardia, or a salad with stephanotis, turkey with a tuberose, or lobster with lily-of-the-valley. If the incongruity seems preposterous the author has suffered acutely from such ignorance enough times to warn the reader against trying to blend flower fragrance and food. If you *must* have flowers on the table choose the scentless kinds or else the milder types of fragrance as listed under 1, 5 and 6 in the first chapter.

As to other rooms in the house there is nothing that needs to restrict the use of fragrant flowers anywhere, except the well-intrenched notion that they should not be left in a sick-room overnight, which is probably a fallacious hangover from the supposed efficacy of flowers as disinfectants! Feminine taste can dispose of fragrance otherwise as she thinks fit, but it should be stressed that of the flowers listed below some are definitely not for the bedroom or boudoir—unless there is still a streak of Cleopatra in her modern sisters. These are all marked [2] or [3] in the list that follows.

FRAGRANT FLOWERS FOR THE HOUSE

We assume that most gardeners will want to use the material they have grown themselves. Hence, all the flowers listed have been already described in Chapters Two, Three, and Four, so that the notes on them will not be repeated here, except as to their utility as cut flowers. No so-called florist's flowers are included, and if the list seems meagre, it should be remembered that only the most outstanding kinds have been included. Wherever known, and for the convenience of those who want to *select* their types of fragrance, each sort has a number written thus [1], [2], etc. Where they are marked with two numbers, it means that they have combined two types of fragrance. Although all these are explained in detail in the first chapter, it is perhaps well to summarize.

TYPES OF FRAGRANCE

1. Aminoid. Type flower, hawthorn. Rather mild, faintly sweet, and disturbing to some.
2. Heavy. Type flower, jasmine. The heaviest, sweetest, and most seductive of all flower odors.
3. Aromatic. Type flower, clove pink. Spicy, aromatic, often vanilla-scented, but many of them so sweet as to merge into Group 2.
4. Violet. Type flower, *Viola odorata*. Milder, often elusive, found in almost no wild violets.
5. Rose. Type flower, the fragrant roses. Spicy, fruity, delicate, and often very sweet.
6. Lemon. Type flower, the four-o'clock. Rather lemony, but sometimes very fragrant as in magnolia and our native white water-lily.

The flowers suitable for the house, their type of fragrance, and the chapter in which further notes on them should be sought follow. (Latin names are used only where necessary.)

CARNATION [3]. Chapter Two, Section 3. Fragrance lasts for several days.

Chimonanthus praecox [3]. Chapter Two, Section 3. Cut twigs, unlike a good many other shrubs, are satisfactory as to fragrance in the house.

DAME'S ROCKET [3]. Chapter Four. Night-flowering, and very spicy.

FLOWERING CURRANT *(Ribes sanguineum)* [3]. Chapter Three, Section 3. More spicily fragrant in the house than outdoors.

Gladiolus tristis [3]. Chapter Four. Night-fragrant and summer-flowering.

HYACINTHS [2] and [3]. Chapter Three, Section 3. All of them with a heavy, rich and spicy fragrance.

JASMINE [2]. Chapter Two, Section 2. Probably, with the tuberose, the most fragrant of all flowers, tending to be most fragrant at night.

JONQUIL [2]. Chapter Three, Section 2. Many think this and the poet's narcissus are too sweet, seductive, and "dangerous" for indoor use.

LAVENDER [3]. Chapter Three, Section 3. Flowers keeping their fragrance, as do the leaves, long after they are dried.

LILAC [2]. Chapter Two, Section 2. Beautiful for a day or two, but soon losing its fragrance.

Magnolia virginiana [6]. Chapter Two, Section 6. A sweet-spicy fragrance. A few flowers will scent up a whole room.

Magnolia stellata [6] and [4]. Chapter Two, Section 6. Very early-flowering variety—often in early April.

MOCK-ORANGE *(Philadelphus coronarius)* [2]. Chapter Two, Section 2. One of the most sweet-smelling of all shrubs, entrancing some and obnoxious to others.

NIGHT-SCENTED STOCK [3] and [2]. Chapter Four. Night-fragrant and so much so that a single stalk to a room is enough.

PEONY [5]. As many peonies are scentless and some actually repulsive, it is best to consult details in Section 5 of Chapter Three before selecting any for indoor fragrance.

POET'S NARCISSUS [2]. Chapter Three, Section 2. As with the jonquil, thought to be too sweet for indoor use. However, the Chinese sacred lily, which is a variety of a related species, is grown by the thousands in pebbles and water by those who do not find its odor too disturbing. It is extremely sweet.

ROSES [5] and [3]. Chapter Two, Section 5. Many tea and hybrid perpetual roses may be faintly fragrant outdoors but develop full sweetness in a room. Dried rose petals retain some of the odor for a considerable time.

SWEET PEA. Chapter Three. Many sweet pea varieties are essentially scentless. See Chapter Three for those that are worth cultivating for fragrance. All of these make fine flowers for cutting.

SWEET PEPPERBUSH *(Clethra alnifolia)* [2] and [3]. Chapter Two, Section 3. Sprays of this shrub in August and September are intensely fragrant,—aromatic with a whiff of lilac.

TUBEROSE [2]. Chapter Three, Section 2. With the jasmine, the sweetest and most alluring of flower scents, especially in the evening.

TULIP [1]. Chapter Three, Section 1. Many tulips are all but scentless outdoors, especially among the Darwin group. But some varieties, in a closed room, develop a delightful fragrance. See Chapter Three for a list of these.

TEA OLIVE *(Osmanthus fragrans)* [2]. Chapter Two, Section 2. Jasmine-like in fragrance, but otherwise not showy. Found only in warmer regions than New York, and in Norfolk blooming in April.

Viburnum carlesi [1] and [2]. Chapter Two, Section 2. Beautifully fragrant sprays of this, by judicious and careful pruning, add a delightfully spicy and sweet odor to any room in April-May.

VIOLET. [4]. Chapter Three, Section 4. Unless you are equipped to grow the florist's violet *(Viola odorata),* one cannot expect much fragrance from any of the wild violets. The florist's violet definitely increases its fragrance indoors.

Any inquisitive and experimental gardener could no doubt find many other plants in Chapters Two, Three, and Four, which are well fitted for cutting and retain their fragrance in a warm room long enough to make them useful. The foregoing list, therefore, does not so much aim at completeness as to suggest basic material for fragrance in the house. Of course, fragrance wafted through open windows is better than any cut flowers, and, for this, certain of the shrubs and vines mentioned in Chapter Two are eminently fitted.

The preservation of fragrant flowers after they have been cut (not pulled or torn loose) is a controversial subject often complicated by considerable chicanery. Various "magic" chemicals are promoted, usually without a formula, doubtfully effective and far too expensive. If anything better than plain water at room temperature (changed every day or so) is needed, there is some evidence that a bit of charcoal will help to maintain freshness. In the case of tulips, one-half ounce of calcium nitrate to about one and one half gallons of water has been recommended, but even this is disputed. Freshness is best enhanced by keeping cut flowers away from a draught, the radiator, and the electric fan.

Chapter Six

Perfume from Your Garden

There is scarcely a woman in the world who does not yearn for the finest, most choice, and incidentally most expensive perfume made by the masters of the art in Grasse. Within this small section of southern France the finest perfumes, and especially the essential ingredients of them, have been manufactured for generations by a few great houses who guard their secrets better than do some governments.

Those secrets, quite simply, are the extraction of fragrance from many of the flowers already mentioned in earlier chapters, the fixing and blending of them, and, in all but the most costly, adding the necessary amount of synthetic material, as well as various oils, gums, and other odorous products, the very names of which stir memories of far-off places. Musk, civet, ambergris, patouchli, rosewood, olibanum, and neroli oil —what they are and where they come from must be left mostly to the economic botanist, for all but the first three are derived from plants.

Although the basis of all good perfumes is the fragrance of various flowers, very few perfumes consist only of this, partly because it would be fantastically expensive, and mostly because few flower scents are lasting enough to make good perfume without fixatives or enhancements or potentiation of the initial fragrance. These are the secrets of the expert perfumer. The basic principles upon which his mastery is based are well known, but there is no use ignoring the fact that a choice perfume is a combination of rare skills in horticulture, organic and synthetic chemistry, manufacturing processes, and just plain know-how.

Let no amateur gardener think for a moment that she can duplicate such creations from her own garden. What can be done, and it will be far better than the cheap 100 per cent synthetic perfumes that flood the market, is to utilize a handful of those basic techniques which, after centuries of trial and error, have solved the problem of putting flower fragrance into a bottle.

This may sound simple enough. But, on second thought, is it? Scents are evanescent, are gone in a day or so, and some, like the violet, are a will-o'-the-wisp and doubly hard to capture. So true is this that a true essence of violet flowers is fabulously expensive. So rare and enchanting is their odor that one easily understands the enthusiast long ago who told the ladies of his day:

> "Rub thy face with violets and goat's milk and there is not a prince in the world who will not follow thee."

Much easier to capture is the heavy, seductive odor of jasmine. Some women in Persia, Arabia, and India found this out long before French perfumers were covering thousands of acres with this most fragrant of all shrubs. The Oriental women rolled up in their well-oiled hair as many jasmine flowers as convenient, for they knew that the oil would extract and hold the fragrance. This was gradually released during the night to make of their hair and skin a ravishment of alluring sweetness.

These Oriental ladies unwittingly discovered a secret that is still the basis of much French perfumery and, as we shall see presently, is about the only technique readily applicable to the home gardener who wants to make her own perfume. Flower scents are captured and held by various techniques, mostly by distillation, by extraction with ether and gasoline, by various systems of macerating the flowers, and by the method found so potent by the amorous ladies of the East.

Distillation is generally impossible for the amateur, and many flower odors are partly destroyed by the heat unless the process is carried out by experts. Maceration and extraction by chemical solvents are also for the professionals. But the extraction of odors by their absorption into oils and fats is perfectly feasible and just as sure as the absorption of jasmine in the well-oiled hair of the girls in Persia.

Every housewife knows to her cost that exposed butter in the refrigerator will absorb the odor of turnips, fish, cheese, and other unwanted scents. To translate that fact into making perfume seems a perfectly obvious step to us, but it took many centuries to make it the art that it has become in France where they call it *enfleurage.*

There is, of course, more to enfleurage than the mere absorption of fragrance by fats. The kind of fat and the kinds of flower odors are essential parts of the technique, but more important still is the method of getting the fragrance from the fat or oil into a bottle. Some of this comprises trade secrets, and still more so are the blending and fixing of the odors in the finished perfume.

The typical enfleurage plant in France will have hundreds (or thousands) of sheets of glass, coated both sides with specially prepared fat, and between the sheets of glass (spaced about 2 inches apart) is placed a layer of flower petals (or whole flowers if they are small). The flowers just fill the space between the glass, and a fresh lot of flowers is put in every day or so, until it is obvious that the fat has absorbed all the odor it will contain. What happens in extracting the fragrance from the fat and making the finished perfume is too complicated to include here, but fortunately for the amateur it is perfectly possible to utilize the principle of enfleurage in making an acceptable home-made perfume—at a cost of almost nothing except time.

FLOWER MATERIALS

In home-made enfleurage the choice of material is limited by the fact that some odors are better outdoors than in, and some, like the violet, are all but impossible to capture. Generally those flowers coming within Types 2 and 3 as to fragrance are the most likely to succeed, and it is advisable to look over Sections 2 and 3 of the second, third, and fourth chapters in order to get an over-all picture of fragrance.

By far the best procedure is to go out in the garden and decide for yourself which of the flower odors you want to preserve. Upon that decision will be based your garden practice for the next season, for few except quite extensive gardens will have enough flowers to make anything but a tiny bottle of the finished perfume. After you have decided what perfume you wish to make, the next step will be to increase your plantings of that variety so that there will be an ample supply when fragrance is at its best. Perennials and annuals will always be the best source of perfume material, for they are the easiest to propagate or restrict as tastes vary.

Although a detailed study of Chapters One to Four will be of the greatest help in making a selection for enfleurage, a few notes may be summarized here as to the most desirable flowers for home-made perfume.

ROSES. Choose dark red, crimson, but not white or pale pink varieties mentioned in Chapter Two, Section 5.

VIOLET. There is little use in attempting this. Most "violet" perfume is synthetic, probably because the extraction of true violet fragrance is fabulously expensive.

JASMINE. Probably the most fragrant shrub known, but of use only to those living south of Norfolk.

TUBEROSE. The basis of much French perfumery and easily grown by anyone. See Chapter Three, Section 2.

CARNATION. The ordinary florist's carnation will do, but it is better to grow your own if in a suitable climate. See Chapter Three, Section 3.

LILY-OF-THE-VALLEY. Easy to propagate and will make large patches with hundreds of blooms in a few years.

HYACINTH. Early and spring-flowering and heavily scented.

LAVENDER. Fresh flowers in midsummer. Useful also because the flowers retain a lot of their scent when dried.

NIGHT-SCENTED STOCK. So fragrant that one will scent up a whole room. Night-fragrant, so that the flowers for enfleurage must be picked at night.

JONQUIL AND POET'S NARCISSUS. Both easily grown and extremely fragrant, some think almost insupportably. The trumpet kinds are useless for fragrance.

MIGNONETTE. Must be cut and used at once as it soon loses its fragrance.

Many others will no doubt suggest themselves as you walk about the garden with a nose tuned not only for outdoor fragrance, but to the possibility of preserving it. Almost any flower will do, but it should be remembered in making a choice that the mild and elusive scents are all but impossible to imprison by enfleurage.

It is essential, also, in collecting flowers for this process to keep a few simple rules in mind.

(a) Collect all day-blooming flowers as soon as the dew is off them.
(b) The cut flowers or separate petals must not be dried out.
(c) Generally, the cut flowers should be brought into a room where the heat will often release additional fragrance. But in no case must it be windy or too hot or dry in the room—a kitchen is ideal.
(d) All outer green parts of the flower, and all green leaves, flower stalks, and stems must be removed. To leave them on invites failure because they start decay.
(e) Pick all rose petals from the flower and throw away all the remnants of the flower.
(f) Night-fragrant flowers must be picked only after dark.

HOME-MADE ENFLEURAGE

Since the basis of enfleurage is fat, it is important to choose the right kinds: it has been found that a mixture of three parts of common beef suet to one part of lard will be the easiest mixture for the amateur. Both of these have a distinctive odor of their own, and it must be removed before anything can be done about bringing flowers and fat together.

To remove the odor it is necessary to put the mixture of lard and suet into a pot which will be three-quarters filled with water, the latter being in the proportion of one quart to a teaspoon of alum. Bring this to a boil and let it boil for a half hour or so. After the fat and water have separated, put in a new lot of water and alum in the same proportion, and again bring it to a boil. Keep on repeating this process until the fat residue is *entirely odorless.*

Then pour off the water and allow the fat to cool, picking out any impurities that are left from the suet. After this cooling and cleaning are completed, the fat is ready for the final stage of enfleurage.

Melt the purified and odorless fat so that it can just be poured, that is, about the consistency of cold molasses. Pour it into soup plates or, if larger quantities of flowers are to be processed, into bigger platters. The important point is that you must have duplicate soup plates or platters, which, if placed upside down together, their rims will engage so that there will be only a minimum of leakage.

While the fat is still soft enough, take a knife and score it, so that it is ultimately criss-crossed with knife impressions to the depth of the fat. You then have two (or twenty if you have enough flowers) soup plates or platters coated on the inside with the scored fat. Allow this to cool and become hard as it will. You are then, and only then, ready to use the petals or flowers of your choice.

Place them as thickly as possible, but not more than two layers deep on one of the fat-lined plates. Upon it, upside down, place the other fat-lined plate. If they are approximately alike in dimensions, the two edges ought to make a reasonably tight seal. If they are not really sealed (that is, if their touching edges permit the escape of too much flower fragrance), seal them with more fat or tire tape.

In about one or at most two days, nearly all the fragrance from the flowers will have been absorbed by the fat. The container then should be opened and a new lot of fresh flowers be put in, with the same precautions to prevent leakage of scent. Repeat the process three or four times, or until it is obvious that the fat has absorbed all the odor it can stand. You are then ready for the next stage of enfleurage.

Remove all the fragrance-impregnated fat from the plates, and chop it up into fine pieces (pea size or smaller). Place them into well-corked or stoppered bottles in the proportion of one half chopped-up fat to one half 90 per cent alcohol by volume. Put the bottle in a dark closet and thoroughly shake it as often as convenient for a period of at least three months. Then strain off the flower-scented alcohol, not with the idea that this is your finished perfume, for it is not. It is only ready for the final stage of the operation.

You are now at the most critical stage of the whole process. Alcohol, being extremely volatile, will if left uncorked evaporate off all the scent it has captured from the fat. To prevent this, and to make your labor produce a first-rate amateur perfume, you must add a fixative. If you are of an experimental turn of mind, any one of several ingredients, none of which comes from your garden, will do.

The best fixatives for the home perfumer are oil of cedar and oil of sandalwood, both of which may be purchased from any good drug store. Whether you use one or the other, and the amount you use of either, will depend on what you want your finished product to smell like. Its initial odor, is, of course, the flower you selected, but both these wood oils have a distinct odor of their own. You can use one or the other, or a combination of both, but the object should be to put in just enough to counteract the volatility of the alcohol without masking the odor of the flowers. Only at this final stage can anyone guess at the right amount of oil of cedar or oil of sandalwood, for it depends on (1) condition of the fragrance when the flower was picked, (2) completely deodorizing the fat before use, and (3) how well it was shaken and stored. A little practice will settle the question. You now have your home-made perfume—except for what the French would consider its most important ingredients.

It should be clearly understood that the amateur perfumer can stop right here and have the fragrance of his choice bottled up in a perfectly acceptable perfume—in fact far better than the plethora of cheap, synthetic substitutes that flood the market. But our home-made product is still far from a blended perfume, and to add the necessary ingredients is both expensive and hazardous. These are civet, musk, and ambergris. We can exclude the last as being so expensive that it is safer to pay the price and buy a bottle of the fine products of France.

Musk and civet, both animal products, are relatively expensive, but they add greatly to any perfume. They can be purchased from dealers in minute amounts and are needed in almost microscopic proportions. The exact amounts only you can tell, for it depends upon the concentration of perfume you have been able to capture and whether it is of the *heavy* or *aromatic* type.

AN EASIER SUBSTITUTE

If all this seems a bit too much trouble and you are satisfied with a somewhat inferior substitute, there is still a way out for the amateur. It involves the same property of fats to absorb odors, but the perfumes made under the process to be noted presently are not as lasting as those prepared by enfleurage. The collection and preparation of the flowers are the same as before, but the operation is much simpler.

Get a good-sized stone or porcelain crock, preferably cylindrical, that is, with straight sides. Put in the bottom a pad of cotton-wool that is soaked in olive oil, or any substitute oil that is essentially odorless. Upon the oil-soaked pad spread a layer of flowers or petals (about three-quarter inch deep) and over them sprinkle a thin layer of common salt (not enough to cover them completely). Put in another oil-soaked pad, which, like the one below and above it, should just touch the sides of the crock. Put in another layer of flowers and salt, and continue the process until the jar is seven-eighths full.

Then press the mass of petals or flowers and oil-soaked pads as much as possible, and leave on the top layer a heavy stone or preferably a piece of lead cut to fit easily inside the crock. After pressing down as much as possible, and leaving the stone or lead to supplement your pressing, tie wax paper over the mouth of the crock and leave it alone, in the shade, for *only two days.*

At the end of the pressing period, open the crock and dump the contents into a porcelain wash basin over which has been stretched a large enough piece of muslin or cheesecloth so that its upturned corners will make a bag holding the entire contents of the crock—of course, suspended over the basin to catch the drops of the fragrant oil. In order to catch all of this oil, it is better to squeeze the bag until there is no more drip.

The basin will then contain your strained and fragrant oil, and in this comparatively simple process you have completed the preparation of your perfume. It will not be so good as that derived from home-made enfleurage, but is an acceptable substitute for it.

Perhaps the amateur perfumer is wondering why no mention has been made of rose water, and attar of roses, which some people prefer to call "otto of roses," although the term *attar* seems more appropriate, since it stems from a Persian word that means perfume, and it was originally from Persia and Arabia that the first attar of roses was produced. Avicenna, a learned Arab physician (A.D. 980-1037) seems to be the first who thought up the idea of *distilling* fragrance, at least three centuries before the distilling of wine to make brandy became common. He was also the first to tell us about coffee.

It is this distilling process which gives us attar of roses. And it takes 180-300 pounds of rose petals to make a single ounce of rose oil which is actually attar of roses. This purest of all rose scents, mostly made from the Damask rose and a variety of *Rosa alba,* is costly and is generally diluted with geranium *(Pelargonium)* and other fragrant leaf oils. In distilling the oil from rose petals there is a large liquid residue, and it is this which is marketed as rose water.

Distilling rose fragrance for attar, and its by-product of rose water is a highly expert job, especially in Bulgaria and France where most of it is produced. Equipment for it is expensive, the amount of petals needed is tremendous, and all this, plus the necessary skills involved, makes attar of roses and rose water a bit impractical for the amateur enthusiast. There are several so-called rose waters concocted by steeping fresh rose petals in wine or alcohol, or by simmering in water, but they are generally rather weak-scented and not worth keeping, for they quickly lose their odor. Oil of rose is precious and gives up its fragrance only to the initiated. Fortunately, however, the oil is not all lost as the petals dry out, which brings us to the preservation of fragrance from dead rose petals and our last chapter.

Chapter Seven

Potpourri and How to Make It

Hundreds of years before America bestowed the fragrance of tobacco smoke upon the Old World, the Europeans had discovered that burning fragrant woods and gums was so pleasurable that not only were ordinary houses fragrant with such smoke, but it was used in their temples. No one smoked pipes, for they were unknown before Columbus, but the ancients developed to a high art the practise of inhaling the fragrant smoke of myrrh and frankincense, burned in braziers. And it was apparently the Jews who bequeathed incense to the Roman Church, which to this day makes their ritual a perfumed rapture to the faithful.

Incense, however, was not always so exalted. It figures in many bacchanalian scenes, for, with various scent pots and sachets, it was an easy way to store and use, when wanted, the fragrance in flowers and many other odorous products of the plant and animal world. Smoke seemed to enhance the enchantment of fragrance, especially before the discovery of distillation of perfumes, which did not come until early in the Tenth Century.

Ever since the days of the Greeks, Romans, and Persians, we have sought various ways of holding the dried fragrance of flowers, usually mixed with other things, without burning them. It is this search that has bequeathed us the potpourri. As here understood it will be confined to the capture of rose scent, which is the easiest and most satisfactory, because rose petals hold some of the fragrant oil in their dried petals, although not much.

One rather critical Englishman sniffs at all potpourris just because of the failure of dried rose petals to hold all the fragrance of the fresh flower. A potpourri today, and always in the past, has many other things added to it to enhance or sometimes even mask what should be the predominant odor of the rose. Because the petals do not hold all their fragrance when dry, it is essential to start with only the most fragrant sorts.

Of these the Damask and Provence roses are, by all means, the best. Of the latter there is a variety known as the Apothecary's Rose *(Rosa gallica officinalis)* which is strongly favored by some writers in England where they are especially proficient in the making of potpourri. That variety is all but unknown in this country, so we must fall back on two of the most fragrant of the old-fashioned roses, the Damask and Provence or, as some call it, the French rose. If none of these is available, choose any of the deep red varieties of hybrid perpetual roses listed among the two dozen kinds found in Section 5 of Chapter Two.

A word now as to the amount of rose petals that is necessary, even for a small potpourri of at least one gallon, as it is useless to go to all the trouble for less than this. You will need, but not necessarily all at once, approximately two gallons of fresh rose petals for the moist variety of potpourri and over twice that amount for the dry method. The latter is easier but not so satisfactory.

For both methods the picking of the flowers is the same, and only roses that are nearly or quite fully open should be chosen —none that have passed their prime. Even more important is the time of day. As all are to be fully or partly dried, and as rapidly as possible, the flowers should never be picked when there is any dew clinging to them, and never for at least a day after the last rain, as the petals hold considerable water for longer than one would suspect. Afternoon picking is the best. As the subsequent handling of the flowers is quite different, the details will be deferred until the dry and moist methods are noted specifically.

The purpose of both is the same, and both should be made in very different containers from those ultimately used to perfume a room. The containers are works of art, especially in France and England—often of china, but many of rare woods, or even of gold and silver. All of the better sort should have a double top, the upper one to screw down tight and keep the fragrance in when not wanted, the lower one with holes or criss-crossed open bars to permit the contents to scent the room.

The containers for making the potpourri must be much stouter than this, for their contents will have to be stirred and sometimes rammed, and some of the ingredients, at least in the moist method, will stain. The most practical type of container is the straight-sided crock, such as our ancestors used for butter or cookies, and it must have a fairly tight-fitting crock top. It is quite useless to use any sort of absorbent container such as unbaked clay, as the inner surface must be glazed. Do not use any metal or enamelled container. Also, before starting, provide yourself with a round, heavy stone (8-10 pounds) or a flat piece of lead that will fit the container like a loose piston-head. This will be needed only for the moist method. You will also need a stout, rounded stick to pound down the petals—a rolling pin, with one handle sawn off will do. Also a stout, wooden spoon should be available. Be careful not to use any metal utensils.

DRY POTPOURRI

The ordinary potpourri of the shops is likely to be merely some dried rose petals to which perfume, usually synthetic, has been added. If one is satisfied with such a concoction, there is no use of going to the trouble of making your own—for even the dry potpourri does take time. Also it should be understood that, although much better than the usual store product, it is not as good as the one made by the more difficult moist method.

As the predominant odor is to be rose, the major part of the jar should be filled with dried rose petals—and they should be perfectly dry. To see that they are dried as quickly as possible, spread the petals on cheesecloth-covered frames so arranged that there is a good circulation of air above and below. Lacking such frames, the petals may be spread thickly on clean, unprinted paper. It is absolutely essential that only the petals are used; all green parts of the flower, stem, etc., will only invite the musty odor of decay.

A foggy or humid day is to be avoided, since the object is to dry the petals thoroughly as quickly as possible; in the sun or in a warm, dry room that should not take more than 24-36 hours. If you do not have enough dried rose petals nearly to fill the gallon crock, store some in the crock for a few days until you have accumulated enough.

Before you begin the mixing of your potpourri, there are some other plants from your garden that should also be picked and dried. Leaves, flower clusters, and herbage generally should have been gathered of any of the following: balm, mint, rosemary, lavender, etc. Or, if you fancy it, any other fragrant leaves such as geranium *(Pelargonium),* verbena, lemon verbena, carnations, etc. How you use these will depend upon your taste in odors, especially how much you want to mask the predominant rose scent. It must be confessed that perfectly dried rose petals do not preserve much of the odor of the fresh flowers—hence the desirability of having the dried leaves of the herbs and also the last ingredients that you must have before you start mixing.

Assuming that you will be starting with about three quarts of dried rose petals (the extra quart will be taken up with the dried leaves mentioned above), you will also need the following ingredients, all of which can be purchased from any good drug or department store.

1/3 ounce of each of the following:
Powdered mace, cloves, cinnamon and allspice.

1/5 ounce of each of the following:
Crushed coriander seeds, crushed cardamon seeds.
Powdered gum storax, powdered gum benzoin.

In addition to these you will need considerable common salt. Some prefer to use sea salt and common salt mixed half and half, but, if sea salt is hard to come by, the common kitchen variety will do.

You are now equipped to mix the potpourri. This is done by putting layers of dried flower petals, leaves, etc., at the bottom of the crock, sprinkling each layer with a little salt and a pinch or two of your ground and mixed spices. Keep on repeating the process—alternate layers of petals, salt, and spices until the crock is filled. Some then prefer to sprinkle about a third of an ounce of brandy over the mixture. Put the top on and leave it for about two weeks. Then give the mixture a thorough stirring, replace the top and stir it at weekly intervals for at least two months. It is then ready to be put in any ornate container, a bit at a time, keeping the stock mixture closely covered.

It must be confessed that such a potpourri, which has been made for centuries by devoted enthusiasts, somewhat justifies the skepticism of that Englishman who wondered whether we liked the odor of spices and herbs better than the rose. Dozens of variations of this recipe from Sir Kenelm Digby's (1603-1665) down to the most recent "discovery" at last week's meeting of the garden club have been published. All of them, if following the dry method, suffer from the fundamental and inescapable fact that rose petals lose far too much fragrance when dry.

Some modern, and quite a few old recipes, admit that dried rose petals are not enough, and to the ingredients already noted they would add small amounts of bay leaves, orange or jasmine blossoms, civet, musk, and even attar of roses! This seems a confession that the dry potpourri with a base of rose petals is very far from providing the bewitching odors of fresh flowers.

MOIST POTPOURRI

The advocates of this method are likely to be a bit scornful of whatever variation of the dry method you favor. They point out, with unimpeachable truth, that too much of the fragrant oil in rose petals is lost by the complete drying necessary for that process. Hence the moist method, which involves only *partial* drying out of the petals, seems to be preferred. The flowers are picked just as in the dry method, but the plucked, fresh petals are managed so that they hold a good deal more of their fragrance.

The object in the moist method is to dry the rose petals only just enough so that they will have lost about half of their juice by evaporation, without losing at the same time too much of the precious fragrant oil. How to tell this? There is no accurate way to do so, but experience does tell us that they are about half dry when the total *bulk* of the collected petals has been reduced by one half.

To the question "Why not reduce the moisture by artificial heat, under controlled conditions?"—the best answer is provided by Nature. Gradual drying in the shade, and preferably out of the wind, will drive off enough moisture without rapid dissipation of fragrance. Any artificial heat would certainly dissipate the fragrance in a few hours. Generally, with average outdoor drying conditions, the petals should be dry enough to use in two days. A good place to dry them would be on a sheet placed where neither rain nor sunshine can hit it. The petals should be about half their size and feel flabby in two days or less if the humidity is low. Only experience will tell you when the petals have reached the right degree of dryness, for petals vary among themselves, especially the water content of different species.

The important thing is to make a decision as to when they are ready and then to act at once. Put a layer of the half dry petals in the bottom of your crock and sprinkle liberally, but do not cover, with salt. Ram and press down the layer, and keep on putting alternate layers of salt and petals until you have used up the current supply. Ram them all down and weight them down with the stone or piece of lead. Leave them alone until you have another supply of half-dried petals. These may be added every few days, being careful about ramming and the weight. Such a well-stuffed crock can be left all summer, with the lid on, and there will be no danger of spoiling if the rose petals are clean of stems, leaves, etc., and there has been a liberal use of salt. Sometimes, if the petals were not quite dry enough, there will be a small accumulation of liquid at the bottom of the crock, and this should be poured away.

In the meantime you should have been getting together the other ingredients that come from the garden, as well as those from more remote sources. For this you will need another crock, about one-half the size of the one in which the rose petals are brewing. Into this put alternate layers of sweet-smelling herbs and salt, just as with the rose petals, but being careful to see that the leaves, herbage, etc., of thyme, balm, rosemary, geranium, basil, verbena, or whatever fragrant materials you gather is only about one-half dry when put into the crock.

The herbs, with a sprinkling of salt between each layer, will ultimately fill the crock, but while they may be pressed down moderately they must not be rammed tight for the good reason that in between each layer of herbs there is another ingredient to be put in that will not stand ramming. This is orange peel.

If you are fortunate enough to be able to get fresh Seville or bitter oranges (possible only in California and Florida), peel them and cut the rind into strips. While still fresh, stud the outer side of each strip with as many cloves as you can, the shanks pricked into the rind so plentifully that the bulbous tips of the cloves are practically touching. If Seville (which is merely another name for the bitter) oranges are not available, get any variety of the common, sweet orange that has a thick rind with plenty of citrus oil in it.

Between each layer of herbs, put a few strips of these clove-studded orange peels, and leave the crock closed until you are ready for the final mixing of your moist potpourri. If the mixture does not shrink down in the crock, as it should, with absorption of moisture by the salt, it is permissible to press it down *gently;* do not ram it. It should be stated perhaps that the salt can be, as in the dry method, half sea salt and half the common sort, or only the latter if sea salt is not available. Neither has any odor, nor do they enhance the odor of any ingredient. The only virtues of the salt, and they are cardinal, are that it is hygroscopic and hence absorbs some of the excess moisture from your materials, without dwindling its fragrance; it also prevents decay. The latter may be serious if you have not been careful about the correct amount of moisture in petals or herbs as they are finally put into the crocks.

With your two crocks brewing, one with rose petals and the other with fragrant herbs, you are now ready to start the final mixing of your moist potpourri and the stage must be set for this before either crock is opened and actual mixing can start. Both the crocks thus may have been brewing from rose-time to autumn, especially if you have waited for the petals of tuberose which some put into the herb pot to make the final mixture a bit more alluring than most potpourris were ever meant to be. After all, the potpourri is an old invention, mostly for the stylized, aristocratic life of the seventeenth, eighteenth, and nineteenth centuries. But there is no law against making them as seductive as the Greeks and Romans made their sachets or incense.

To finish the job, whether your mixture is elegantly scented or frankly has a touch of what disturbed Socrates twenty-four centuries ago, you must collect and prepare rather carefully the following:

1 ounce of each of the following, finely ground: cloves, mace, allspice, and orris root.
1 ounce of whole mace and whole cloves.
2 ounces of gum benzoin, well pounded.
2 ounces of gum storax, well pounded.

Thoroughly mix all the powdered material in a basin, to which can be added the pounded benzoin and storax, which should also be thoroughly mixed with the spices. Keep in a separate dish the whole mace and cloves. It is permissible, if you are affluent, to add to the basin of powdered spices a minute amount (just a pinch or two) of civet, musk, or ambergris, all of them animal products and far more expensive than all the rest of the ingredients combined. Some, also, put in the shavings or sawdust of sandalwood, but these, too, are expensive and not always easy to come by. It is almost axiomatic that this mixture of fragrant spices should not be made until you are actually ready for the final stage of moist potpourri.

By this time the contents of both crocks should have shrunk by about one half, the rose crock, from pounding and the weight, by even more than this. It will also be packed enough so that it needs a stout fork to loosen it up.

Use a large sheet of clean, unprinted paper or a sheet upon which to mix the ingredients, or it can be done on a clean kitchen table (wood or plastic). The mixing should not be hurried, for it involves not only thorough blending of the ingredients, but also a final period of exposure to the air (to reduce some residual moisture) before packing it away for ultimate use.

To ensure a complete mixture of the four ingredients (rose, herbs, ground spices, and whole ones), take 3 cups of rose and spread upon the mixing table, add 1 cup of the herb mixture, spread as evenly as possible. Over this sprinkle a little of the spice mixture, and add at random a few whole mace and cloves. Keep on doing this until all the crocks and basins are empty and you have stratified layers of rose, herbs, spices, etc. Then the whole mass must be mixed with the greatest of care, either by shovelling it first in one direction and then in another, or better yet with your two hands. It is impossible to mix it too much, after which it should be rammed back into the larger crock, or, if there is any left over, into the smaller one. Both should be well covered (not air-tight) and stood in a cool, dry place. Avoid the heat and dryness of an ordinary steamheated room—under the kitchen sink or in a cellar or garage will be ideal.

Some quite expert makers of potpourri prefer the final storage to be in a keg made of cedar or other fragrant wood, with a well-fitted head—not unlike the small, brass-bound kegs sold for keeping ice cubes. The only real argument for these is that, if used year after year, they absorb and hold some of the fragrance of their contents, and perhaps impart to future ingredients the aroma of the past.

It is the fragrance of May and June, of rose-time, lavender-time and thyme-time, with all the other garden scents, which we seek to capture in a potpourri. Let no one ever think that any potpourri, no matter how carefully made, is better than the fresh flowers, but it does raise grateful memories of them on winter evenings, when flowers are scarce and we crave a breath of what Shakespeare called "a strange, invisible perfume"—for a potpourri is just that, hidden in its magic container.

SACHETS

The material for these scented favorites of the wardrobe are usually artificially blended, scented powders, with all the handicaps as to odor and lasting quality that accrue from such products. Herb gardeners and those devoted to fragrance in the garden can easily make better ones at home.

In making a potpourri, whether you use the dry or moist method, your end-product has captured the fragrance of the garden in at least a semi-permanent form. It is this fragrance that you need in a sachet, which is merely a powdered form of potpourri's material put in whatever container you choose, which, of course, must be porous enough to release the scent.

Other combinations can be made by slowly drying the leaves of lavender, rose-geranium, sage, thyme, rosemary and any other of the fragrant-leaved herbs, which are treated in the companion volume *Herbs in the Garden.* To the powdered leaves one can add pinches of such spices as ground allspice, cloves, cinnamon, or ginger to make whatever combination of fragrance you prefer.

Blending sachet materials is perfectly simple if your plant materials are dry enough to be powdered and fragrant enough to last from one season to the next.

Bibliography

FOX, HELEN M.
Gardening with herbs for flavor and fragrance. 334 pages.
The Macmillan Co., New York, 1933.

HAMPTON, F. A.
The scent of flowers and leaves. 135 pages.
Dulau and Co., London, 1925.

MCDONALD, DONALD
Fragrant flowers and leaves. 136 pages.
Frederick Warne and Co., London, 1905.

ROHDE, ELEANOR S.
The scented garden. 311 pages.
Hale, Cushman and Flint, Boston, 1932.

THOMPSON, C. J. S.
The mystery and lure of perfume. 247 pages.
John Lane the Bodley Head, London, 1927.

VERILL, A. H.
Perfumes and spices, 304 pages.
L. C. Page and Co., Boston, 1940.

WILDER, LOUISE B.
The Fragrant Path. 407 pages.
The Macmillan Co., New York, 1932.

INDEX